THE IRON TSAR

The Life and
Times of John Hughes

Roderick Heather

en Press

First published in Great Britain by Pen Press

All paper used in the printing of this book has been made from wood grown in managed, sustainable forests.

ISBN13: 978-1-907499-17-3

Printed and bound in the UK
Pen Press is an imprint of Indepenpress Publishing Limited
25 Eastern Place
Brighton
BN2 1GJ

A catalogue record of this book is available from the British Library

Cover design by Jacqueline Abromeit

Contents

Notes for the Reader

Currencies and Conversions

During the period of this book, the British currency system was £1 divided into 20 shillings with each shilling divided into 12 pence (£1 = 240 pence). The Russian currency was one rouble divided into 100 kopeks. I have used an exchange rate of eight roubles = one British pound, although the actual rate varied and at times was as high as ten roubles to the pound. Where I have provided a conversion of historic pound amounts into present day (2007) values, I have used the RPI (retail price index) for prices of goods and services and for all other amounts I have used a GDP (gross domestic product) adjusted index. There are other ways of doing these calculations, particularly for wages (based on the average earnings index) but I feel the two indices used most accurately reflect the true underlying change in monetary values for the amounts in this book. For those readers wishing to look in more detail at this subject, there are various internet sites that provide historic currency conversions.

Weights and Measures

The Russian Empire used its own system of weights (the pood or pud – a little over 36 pounds or 16 kilos) and measurement of distances (the verst – roughly one kilometre or 0.625 of a mile). Where I have used or quoted contemporary sources, some of these referred to the old British ton (2240 pounds). I have therefore converted these using the current British measure of metric tonnes (2200 pounds).

Russian Spelling
Over the years, the names of several towns and cities mentioned in this book have changed and in such cases I have used the names that were in use at the time. For all Russian and Ukrainian names, locations and words, I have tried to use the currently accepted Anglicised version. For consistency, I have also used the Anglicised version of Russian names or locations rather than any alternative Ukrainian spelling. Since the Russian alphabet has no letter 'H' various transliterations have been used over the years for the name of the town that John Hughes established. Depending on the source quoted, the reader will find mention of Yusovka, Iuzovka and Hughesoffka but for my own writing, I have elected to go with Hughesovka in this book out of respect for its founder.

I fully acknowledge that all errors of calculation or interpretation are mine.

I gratefully acknowledge the cooperation of the Glamorgan Records Office in Cardiff in providing access to their John Hughes archive and their kind permission to use some of its photographs which are indicated by (GRO) in the relevant captions.

PREFACE

For most people today that live outside the former Soviet Union, the country of Ukraine is relatively unfamiliar. If asked what they know about the Ukraine, the responses would probably be fairly limited. There might be a vague understanding that it lies close to Russia and the Black Sea. Some might mention its Orange Revolution in 2004 or its surprising success in the Eurovision Song Contest of the same year. Others might have heard of a couple of its football teams or tennis players. And that would probably be it for most people. In the mid-19th century, the level of knowledge of the Ukraine was even less. In an age when the Victorians and their empire were increasingly expanding across the world on the back of trade and industry, the names of far-flung places in the Far East, India, North America and Africa were much more familiar to most people. Even the locations of battles in the recent Crimean War were unlikely to be associated in their minds with a country we now call the Ukraine. Yet for John Hughes and his family, the Ukraine and Russia were to become intimately familiar. It would be his new life and ultimately, where he died.

In 1870, having worked his way up from humble beginnings in South Wales, John Hughes although only semi-literate, was a successful inventor, wealthy industrialist and family man living in London. At the age of 55 he decided to leave everything behind and move to the desolate Ukrainian Steppe, then part of Tsarist

Russia, to set up a modern iron and steel works. Having negotiated a contract with the Russian government and raised the capital in England to finance the new enterprise, he set sail for the Ukraine. He took with him not only all the equipment necessary to establish a complete ironworks, but also much of the skilled labour to build and run it – a group of about a hundred ironworkers and miners mostly from South Wales. Within a few years, despite the extremely difficult conditions, they succeeded in building the most modern industrial complex in Russia, including coal and iron ore mines, blast furnaces and brickworks plus their own railway lines, and became a leading supplier of rails for Russia's expanding railroad system.

Faced with an acute labour shortage in the area, Hughes built a town to attract workers from all over Russia. The settlement that he founded around the works became known as Hughesovka and the company built housing for all its workers as well as schools, churches, hospitals, shops and even a brewery. Later joined by his four sons, the company grew and prospered, becoming one of the country's largest and most profitable enterprises. It led the way in introducing industrial capitalism to Russia with the latest iron and steel manufacturing processes as well as modern mining techniques plus improved working practices, worker safety and welfare. In the 1890s the company was the largest steel producer in Russia employing over 10,000 workers and the town had a population of 30,000. The business and social model introduced by Hughes became an example that was to be adopted by other Russian and foreign companies that followed him to the Ukraine. In the 20th century, despite wars, economic downturns, cholera epidemics and the 1905 revolution the company and town continued to grow. By 1918 the town had a population of 55,000 with close to 20,000 company employees and its value in today's terms stood at over £520 million. But in that year the Bolsheviks seized all the company's assets, booting out the foreigners and the shareholders lost everything. Although the name of Hughes was largely removed from the annals of Soviet history, the factories and mines that he had founded continued in production after the revolution, as they still do to this day. The town of Hughesovka was renamed Stalino in 1921 and then changed again in 1961 to become the modern Ukrainian city of Donetsk with a population today of around one and a half million people.

Interwoven with the story of Hughes and his company there are links with some of the most famous people of the time, including British entrepreneurs such as Brassey, Whitworth, Gooch and Brunel and in Russia, Tsar Alexander II, Lenin and Khrushchev. Hughes' contribution to industrialising the Ukraine and modernising Tsarist Russia was enormous and has largely been unrecognised in his home country. He wasn't the father of the Industrial Revolution in Russia but he was surely one of its most influential uncles. This is the remarkable story of the life and times of John Hughes, his company, fellow workers and the town that he founded.

John Hughes in 1894 *(GRO)*

CHAPTER ONE
The Early Years

John Hughes was born into an era of dramatic changes in Britain. These were changes that would ultimately affect virtually everyone in the country and eventually the rest of the world too. The Industrial Revolution that had started in Britain in the 18th century was gathering pace rapidly. The social and technological changes that occurred in its wake would form the backdrop for Hughes' life and career. There is little documentary evidence relating to John Hughes' early years. Born in Merthyr Tydfil in South Wales, with different sources giving his date of birth as 1814 or 1815, he was one of three children with a younger brother called James and a sister Ann. Hughes did not receive any formal schooling but was educated at home, which was typical for working class families at this time. In his early teens, he then took up an apprenticeship at the nearby Cyfarthfa ironworks, where his father was an engineer. As a skilled employee in a busy works, Hughes' father would have earned a decent wage, sufficient to provide a home and the basic comforts for his family. Hughes completed his apprenticeship at Cyfarthfa, staying for around ten years and this is where he learnt the fundamental skills of ironworking, developing an intimate knowledge of the production process that would serve him for the rest of his life. In order to fully understand Hughes' later achievements and his impact on the world, we need to understand the world in which he grew up and its impact on him. Specifically, we need to briefly look at the growth of industrialisation in Britain and in particular in South Wales.

The first half of the 19th century saw rapid industrialisation in several parts of Britain, based primarily on the new industries of coal, iron and cotton textiles. As the Industrial Revolution took hold, Britain's population exploded, growing from less than nine million in the very first 1801 census to 18 million in 1851 and more than 22 million in 1871. Virtually all the growth took place in towns that just a few decades earlier were quiet small villages and despite Malthus' dire projections about the risks of overpopulation, the standard of living for most people had improved too. However, problems associated with urban poverty and overcrowding were rising. By the early 1840s, Liverpool and Manchester were the most densely populated urbanised areas in the world. The average population density for England and Wales was 275 persons per square mile, whereas the figure for Liverpool was over 138,000 with some parts of the city holding the equivalent of three or four times this number of people per square mile.

By 1850, Britain was producing 56 million tonnes of coal and two million tonnes of pig iron – half the world's output – with 25% exported. In the areas where the iron and coal industry had sprung up, the landscape changed dramatically and new man-made features now dominated the scene. Slag heaps from mining appeared and then steadily grew, along with smoking chimneys. The machinery and equipment of industrial activity spread out across former green fields. The clang of metal beating, the roar of the furnace and the hiss of steam replaced traditional rural natural sounds, whilst coal smoke brought acrid pollution of the atmosphere and became the primary smell in many towns.

In Wales, an abundance of iron ore, limestone, water and wooded valleys for fuel, meant iron making was initially the dominant

2

industry. Ironworks grew up in the valleys running south from the Brecon Beacons particularly around the town of Merthyr. As the forests were depleted, charcoal was replaced as the primary fuel by the new technology of coal. Iron production then spread westwards to the areas around Neath and Swansea where anthracite coal was already being mined. In the 1840s coal mining expanded into the Aberdare and Rhondda valleys. New techniques enabled the use of coal in the form of coke in iron smelting. The canals and growing rail network allowed production to be moved easily to the towns or coast for export. In 1840 more than four million tonnes of coal were produced with over two million tonnes going to the steel industry, one million to the domestic market and other industries and 750,000 tonnes for export. Just 14 years later, eight million tonnes were produced, with two and a half million tonnes exported.

By 1874, Welsh coal production had reached 16 million tonnes, with a quarter of that figure exported. The rise of the coal industry in Wales seemed unstoppable, with high quality coal available in massive quantities. At its peak in 1913, Wales accounted for 20% of coal production in Britain with some 70% exported, more than any other British coalfield. The coal mines were privately owned throughout the 19th century. It was viewed as an area of industry with potentially huge rewards for the investors and speculators, who obtained licences to sink shafts or expand existing mines. Welsh coal had become the fuel of choice for steam boilers worldwide. Smoking chimneys joined colliery winding gear to dominate the growing rows of terraced housing built in the Welsh valleys for immigrant workers from all around Britain.

In terms of iron production, the importance of Wales to the British economy matched its position in coal. In 1840, Wales produced over half a million tonnes, which was 36% of Britain's total output. By 1860, Welsh production had virtually doubled, much of it coming from Merthyr and Dowlais. The subsequent introduction of the new open-hearth furnace invented by Sir William Siemens, which John Hughes was to subsequently adopt in Russia, raised productivity still further.

This industrialisation led to a rapid increase in the population of Wales, like many other parts of the UK, initially largely due to internal migration than to high birth rates. In 1801 just over 587,000 people lived in Wales; by 1901, this had increased to over two million with the largest rises in population in the industrial counties. Large numbers of immigrants arrived from many parts of Britain to find work in the mines and factories of Wales. With the increasing levels of coal and iron passing through the docks, Cardiff, Swansea and Newport experienced huge population growth during the 19th century. The 19th century witnessed a transition from a society that was predominantly rural (around 80% lived outside urban settlements in 1800) to a largely urbanised, industrial society. By the start of the 20th century only 20% of the population in Wales lived in non-urban areas.

The miners and their families faced a difficult new life. Thousands of miners died as a result of roof falls and underground explosions and many more were injured. The terrible working conditions experienced by the miners eventually forced the British government to take action and in 1842 the employment of women and young children in mines was forbidden. Government inspectors had found that children as young as six years of age were working 12-hour shifts underground. The younger children were used to operate mine ventilation systems while older children and women hauled the coal from the face to the bottom of the mine shaft. The owners took little heed of the law, however, and a female worker was killed underground as late as 1866. Above ground, poor housing, overcrowding and unsanitary conditions led to disease and low life expectancy. Many of the small two or three-bedroom properties housed three or four families and if there was a toilet, this would be a shared one between three or four cottages. This lack of basic sanitary requirements led to three cholera epidemics, occurring in the hot summers of 1849, 1854 and 1866. In the 1849 outbreak, more than 800 people died from outbreaks in Merthyr, Dowlais and Aberdare.

Merthyr Tydfil means Tydfil the Martyr in Welsh and was named after Tydfil, a Welsh princess said to have been murdered for her Christian beliefs in 480 AD. But the town in which Hughes grew up was an entirely different place from that of the early Welsh princess. In 1750 Merthyr Tydfil was still a quiet, rural village surrounded by green fields. Most of the 40 or so families who lived in the village worked on the land. By the time of Hughes' birth however, this situation had altered dramatically. Following the discovery that coke could be used for smelting iron, Merthyr Tydfil, with its large supplies of iron ore, coal, limestone and water was an attractive site for this new industry. The first ironworks was opened in 1759. Others followed and by 1784 there were four large ironworks within a two-mile radius of the original village. As these works were established, along with their associated iron ore and coal mines, Merthyr grew from a village of some 700 inhabitants to a large industrial town. The 1801 census recorded a population in Merthyr of over 7700 and by now it was the most populous single parish in Wales. By 1831 the number of inhabitants had grown to 60,000 – more than Cardiff, Swansea and Newport combined.

Small-scale ironworking and coal mining had been carried out in South Wales since the Tudor period, but in the wake of the Industrial Revolution the demand for iron led to the rapid expansion of Merthyr. The ironworks founded by what would become the Dowlais Iron Company in 1759, were the first major works in the area. It was followed in 1765 by the Cyfarthfa where John Hughes worked and later the Plymouth ironworks. A fourth major ironworks, Penydarren, was built by members of the Homfray family in 1784. The Cyfarthfa ironworks were later leased by Richard Crawshay in 1786, and in 1794 he became the sole owner. The ironworks grew rapidly, producing iron that was made into armaments such as cannons. These were in great demand during the late 18th century, especially by the Royal Navy, which needed guns for their ships to protect the steadily expanding British Empire. In 1802, Admiral Lord Nelson visited Merthyr to witness cannons being made for the navy. The manufacture of weapons was so important to the success of the works that the Crawshay family included a pile of cannon balls in their family crest. The early success of the Cyfarthfa works was greatly assisted by the construction of the Glamorganshire Canal in 1794. With its northern terminus at the works the canal linked Cyfarthfa with the port of Cardiff, allowing its products to be transported by sea much more cheaply and quickly than had been possible before. Later the increasing development of railways, both in Britain and overseas, provided an additional rapidly growing market. Several railway companies established routes that linked Merthyr with Welsh coastal ports and other parts of Britain. They often shared routes to enable access to coal mines and ironworks through rugged country, which presented great engineering challenges. Hughes would have seen this new railway engineering work going on around him and as Cyfarthfa provided many of the iron rails, he may well have met or known some of the engineers who were involved. His knowledge of railway construction that he was to later put to good use in the Ukraine probably derived from this time.

Although Stevenson's Rocket which ran from Stockton to Darlington in North-East England is usually considered to have been the very first railway service in the world, in fact the first locomotive to haul a load on tracks ran from the Penydarren ironworks in Merthyr to Abercynon. This was in February 1804 some 20 years before Stevenson's Rocket and it carried 70 passengers and several tonnes of iron.

At the beginning of the 19th century, the Cyfarthfa works employed 1,500 people and it was the largest in the world. At its peak there were up to seven blast furnaces in production, generating great wealth for its owners, the Crawshay family. Richard Crawshay was one of the 50 richest men in the country when he died in 1810. Control of the Cyfarthfa ironworks was passed on in the Crawshay family from father to son for several generations. By the second quarter of the 19th century, the rival ironworks at Dowlais, owned by the Guest family, caught up with and eventually eclipsed the Cyfarthfa works. The early Victorian age witnessed these two great rivals producing enormous quantities of iron rails for the rapidly expanding railway networks in Britain, Europe, America and the colonies of the British Empire. In the 1840s, there were extensive shipments to Russia and a representative of the Russian Tsar once visited Merthyr Tydfil's ironworks because of its important role in supplying iron rails. In 1844 alone, 45,000 tonnes of rails left Merthyr's ironworks to enable expansion of the railways in Russia.

During the first half of the 1800s, the ironworks at Dowlais and Cyfarthfa continued to expand but as development increased, the supply of fresh water in Merthyr Tydfil became extremely poor. The River Taff ran through the town, but the ironmasters diverted the water to supply their steam engines. The Taff became an open sewer and the contaminated water supply resulted in several outbreaks of cholera and typhoid. By 1848 Merthyr's mortality rate was the highest in Wales and the third highest in Britain. The suffering endured by these early ironworkers and their families in South Wales and indeed by the thousands of miners employed in the numerous collieries and factories across Britain can only be imagined. However, despite this high mortality rate, the population of Merthyr continued to grow and reached 40,000 by 1845.

The harsh working conditions were an important contributor to the Merthyr riots in 1831, which John Hughes would have been aware of as a young man. The riots took place at a time of general discontent and demand for reform in South Wales. Three years of depression in the iron industry caused the Merthyr Tydfil iron-masters to make many workers redundant and cut the wages of those in work. Against a background of rising prices this caused severe hardship for many of the working people of the area and, in order to survive, many were forced into debt. The riots were precipitated by a combination of the lack of work, hatred for the courts and bailiffs responsible for the collection of debts and the imposition of factory truck shops. Instead of using normal coin of the realm, some ironmasters paid their workers in specially minted coins or credit notes, known as 'truck'. These could only be exchanged at shops owned by the ironmasters. As with similar company-owned stores the world over, many of the workers understandably objected not only to the principle of truck shops but also to the high prices and low quality of the goods sold. Even when the quality of products for sale in company shops was as good as local market shops, the prices charged could often be more than 20% higher. The following table[1] provides a comparison of prices recorded in 1830 in company truck shops in Monmouthshire, South Wales, compared with those in ordinary market shops –

	Market Shop	Company Shop
Flour, per pack	=2/4d	=2/6d
Bacon, 4 lb	=2/0d	=3/0d
Mutton, 2 lb	=10d	.=1/0d
Beef, 2 lb	=8d	=11d
Sugar, 1 lb	=8d	= 9d
Butter, 1 lb	=9d	=1/0d
Tea, 2 oz	=8d	= 1/0d
Cheese, 2 lb	=1/0d	=1/6d
Totals	=8s.11d	= 11s. 8d

There is still controversy over what actually precipitated the unrest and who was to blame. It became more of an armed rebellion

1   Monmouthshire Merlin, March 1830

than an isolated riot. The initiators were most probably the skilled workers; men who were much prized by the owners and often on friendly social terms with them. They in turn valued their loyalty to the owners and looked aghast at the idea of forming trade unions to demand higher wages. Indeed, the early demonstrations were actually supported by some of the ironmasters. But events overtook them, and the community was tipped into rebellion and despite the hope that they could negotiate with the owners, the skilled workers lost control of the movement.

Local magistrates and police took fright at the growing challenge to their authority and called on the military for assistance. Soldiers were sent from local garrisons but were initially disarmed or turned back by the rioters. Some 10,000 to 12,000 workers marched under a red flag, which was later adopted internationally as the symbol of the working classes. For four days, they effectively controlled Merthyr. But as more troops arrived, they were unable to effectively oppose disciplined soldiers for very long, even with their numbers and captured weapons. The riot was put down without significant bloodshed. Several leaders of the riots were arrested and one was eventually tried and executed. Some were transported as convicts to the penal colonies of Australia.

The first trade unions, which were illegal and savagely suppressed, were formed shortly after the riots. Many families had had enough of the strife and poor living conditions and they left Wales to utilise their skills elsewhere. Some migrated to other parts of Great Britain to find work. Large numbers emigrated by ship to America, where the steelworks of Pittsburgh were booming. History does not record Hughes' reaction to these riots but it is likely they made a strong impression on him. Good management of the workforce was to later become an important issue for Hughes in Hughesovka and where he would have his own strikes and riots to deal with.

In 1850 there were 41 blast furnaces in the Merthyr area, operating day and night with only the occasional shutdown for maintenance and cleaning. The continuous heat and noise emanating from the ironworks made daily life for the inhabitants very stressful as well as unhealthy. Daylight was replaced at sunset not by darkness but by the light and flashes of all the furnace fires and the glow of the smouldering slag heaps. Two contemporary descriptions of Merthyr in 1848 give a clear idea of what it was like –

'The scene at night is beyond conception; the immense fires give a livid hue to the faces of the workmen, and cause them to present a most ghastly appearance; while sounds of blast and steam, rolling mills, and massive hammers worked by machinery or wielded by the brawny arms of athletic sons of Vulcan, preclude the possibility of being heard when speaking.' [2]

The following is a quote from a visitor to the Merthyr area in 1848 called Charles Cliffe:

'The vivid glow and roaring of the blast furnaces near at hand – the lurid light of distant works – the clanking of hammers and rolling mills, the confused din of massive machinery – the burning headlands – the coke hearths, now if the night be stormy, bursting into sheets of flame, now rapt in vast and impenetrable clouds of smoke – the wild figures of the workmen, the actors in this apparently infernal scene – all combined to impress the mind of the spectator wonderfully.' [3]

By 1857 the Dowlais Iron Company had constructed the world's most powerful rolling mill and the company then employed 7,300 people, with probably more than 20,000 people in the town dependent on the works for their livelihoods. Together with the Cyfarthfa works, they were the largest and most productive ironworks in any country, making Merthyr the iron capital of the world. But the good times were not to last. Although new coal mines had been sunk nearby to both feed the work's voracious furnaces and for export, such large quantities of iron had been produced in

---

2   T E Clark – A Guide to Merthyr Tydfil and The Traveller's Companion, 1848

3   Richard Hayman – Working Iron in Merthyr Tydfil, 1989

Merthyr that even before the mid-19th century, local ore supplies were dwindling. The industry became increasingly dependent on imports from abroad which pushed up the cost of making iron products in South Wales. With increasing competition from large, new ironworks overseas, Merthyr's competitive advantage was reduced and it lost many of its foreign markets. By the early 1870s it was clear that the market was also changing. Steel was replacing iron and Merthyr's ironworks could only continue by investing in new technology and converting to steel production. Unfortunately, Cyfarthfa was slow to do this, unlike the rival Dowlais works, only making the change to steel in 1882 after an eight-year period of closure and it lost its former leading position amongst Merthyr Tydfil's ironworks. With the changeover to steel, exports picked up again for a while, especially to Russia and an order for 50,000 tonnes of rails was completed at Merthyr in 1884. But Crawshay eventually ceased trading in 1889 and the end for the Cyfarthfa works finally came in 1919 with most of the works being subsequently demolished.

Largely as a result of the serious health problems in the area, the first Board of Health in England and Wales was established in Merthyr Tydfil in 1851, a precursor of the British National Health Service.

This then was the environment in which Hughes grew up and spent the first part of his working career. His time in Merthyr and at the Cyfarthfa works left a lasting impression on him and as we will see later, there would be several parallels with his Russian enterprise. He witnessed great changes resulting from intense industrial development and massive population growth in the area bringing exciting new opportunities and the creation of considerable wealth. He also experienced cholera outbreaks, riots and other serious social issues that came with industrial progress. Hughes clearly learnt much from the extraordinary events that were going on around him which were to be useful to him later both in Millwall and in Russia. As an intelligent man, it is also highly likely that the social changes and problems he saw made an impact on the development of his own thinking and approach to business. Social attitudes in Britain at the time were governed by what came to be known as the Victorian set of values. Lord Palmerston, Britain's prime minister in the mid-Victorian era, said –

'We have shown the example of a nation, in which every class of society accepts with cheerfulness the lot which Providence has assigned to it; while at the same time every individual of each class is constantly striving to raise himself in the social scale – not by injustice or wrong, not by violence or illegality, but by preserving good conduct, and by the steady and energetic execution of the moral and intellectual faculties with which his creator has endowed him.'

Palmerston felt that in Britain it was possible to reconcile economic change and individual mobility with traditional social balance and stability. For the Victorians, work was not only a means to earn money, respectability and success but also a supreme virtue, involving both self-denial and creative accomplishment. However, this self-help or self-improvement philosophy simply failed to recognise the drudgery of the vast majority of industrial jobs and the impact on workers and their families of related sickness as well as death and injury. Although Hughes was in many ways a typical Victorian entrepreneur and there are certainly echoes of Palmerston's views in his later approach to running his business in Russia, Hughes was to prove that he understood social balance and stability also required pro-active intervention in regard to workers' welfare.

Hughes was clearly able and ambitious, even at a relatively young age. To further his career and gain more experience, he moved on from Cyfarthfa, going first to the Ebbw Vale ironworks, which at that time was well equipped and had started to supply rails for the Liverpool and Manchester railway and the Stockton & Darlington railway. Then in the early 1840s, Hughes moved on to the Uskside Engineering Works in Newport, Monmouthshire. While at the Uskside works, he married. His wife, Elizabeth Lewis was the daughter of the landlord of the Tredegar Arms, which was next door to Uskside and supplied the workers with beer. They lived near the works and had eight children, six boys and two girls, all born in Newport.

By 1852, Hughes' growing capabilities took him to the position of works manager, effectively running Uskside. He now had the opportunity to develop his ideas and interests further and it was at this time that his interest in steam engines developed. He also expanded his skills into foundry work and marine engineering. Although Uskside had begun as a smithy, it had later developed a range of colliery engines and winding gear. With the growth of sea-borne trade through Newport, it had also started to specialise in ship's equipment, anchors and chains. This activity introduced Hughes to the dockyards plus the needs of the maritime world. During his time at Uskside, Hughes patented several inventions relating to armaments, in particular a system of armour plating. His reputation at Newport grew rapidly and his capability became well known in the marine industry worldwide.

It was this fame that brought him into contact with Millwall in London, which was the leading shipbuilding and ironworks centre in Britain. Leaving the valleys of South Wales and relocating his whole family to London must have been a difficult decision for Hughes. It was an important step up in his career and took him into a significantly different world. London was then the epicentre of the vast British Empire and Britain was the workshop of the world, having become the first economic superpower. London was the biggest port in the world and the city was at the heart of world trade, where fortunes and reputations were being made – and lost. To have made such a move Hughes must have been both ambitious as well as confident in his own abilities as well as determined to further his career. This was an auspicious decision by him that ultimately was to open up the way for his move to Russia.

In the mid-19th century, the name Millwall was associated world-wide with the most advanced engineering of the day. Located at Burrell's Wharf on the Isle of Dogs in the Thames, the original Millwall shipbuilding and ironworks was established in 1835 by Sir William Fairbairn, a leading Victorian structural engineer. It seems likely that Hughes' initial job in the Millwall area was as manager of the forges and rolling mills of a company called CJ Mare. This business subsequently became part of Millwall Ironworks & Shipbuilding Company (the company founded by Fairbairn) and by the early 1860s Hughes had earned a place on the board. As a result of the London financial crash of 1866 this business went into liquidation and was broken up into miscellaneous wharves and works. The Millwall ironworks was salvaged from the wreckage and Hughes took over as director and general manager.

Sir William Fairbairn was born in Scotland and came to England to establish an ironworks in Manchester to manufacture mill machinery, ships and steam engines, building the world's first iron-hulled steamship the Lord Dundas. He then moved to London to expand his shipbuilding activities, setting up a shipyard in Millwall in 1835. He was the first to bring iron shipbuilding to the Thames and became a pioneer in the use of iron in the construction of ships. Later, as a consultant to Robert Stephenson on his Conway and Menai Straits bridges in North Wales, it was Fairbairn who conceived the idea of using tubular steel as a construction material to bridge the large gap. He conducted tests to prove this design was both stronger and lighter than solid steel. From 1861 to 1865 he led a government committee to examine the application of iron for defensive purposes and he received a baronetcy in 1869.

It is also interesting to note that the first iron plating for a building also seems to have been manufactured in Millwall back in 1839. In his lecture 'The progress of engineering', Sir William Fairbairn claimed 'It is now twenty years since I constructed an iron house for Halil Pasha, then Seraskier of the Turkish army at Constantinople. I believe it was the first iron house built in this country; and it was constructed at the works in Millwall'.

The iron and shipbuilding industry started by Fairbairn on the Thames grew rapidly over the next 25 years. Together with the nearby Thames ironworks, Millwall formed the largest concentration of privately owned shipbuilding and engineering facilities in Britain. Between them, they built many of the largest and most famous ships of the 19th century. Perhaps the most well known was Isambard Brunel's ill-fated SS *Great Eastern* for which Millwall produced many of the steel plates. Whether Hughes met Brunel is not known but as a senior manager in the company supplying the plates, it is highly likely that Hughes would have had dealings with him. With his keen interest in marine engineering, he would surely have visited the nearby dock where the largest ship in the world was being built.

The *Great Eastern* was conceived as the biggest steamship yet to be built, one that would be capable of carrying 4,000 passengers at a time on a non-stop trip to Australia. The ship, originally called *Leviathan*, was to be nearly 700 feet (over 213 metres) long, six times the size of the largest ship built to date. Brunel designed her to be unsinkable, extending the watertight double plating to 5 feet above the ship's deepest load line with iron bulkheads dividing the ship into 10 watertight compartments. The *Great Eastern* was the first ship to incorporate the double-skinned hull, a feature that would not be seen again in a ship for 100 years. Brunel entered into a partnership with John Scott Russell, an experienced naval architect and ship builder, to construct the *Great Eastern*. But it was a partnership that was to be fraught with problems. Unknown to Brunel, Russell was in considerable financial difficulties. There were disagreements about overall responsibilities as well as many of the project details.

The keel was laid down on May 1, 1854 and she was finally launched after many technical problems on January 31, 1858. It was Brunel's final great project, and he collapsed from a stroke after being photographed on her deck and died only ten days later. The ship was originally designed for the Southampton to New York run, and her 11-day maiden voyage began on June 17, 1860, with 35 paying passengers, 8 company officials 'dead heads' (passengers who don't pay) and 418 crew. But she proved to be uneconomical to use on this route and the ship was later sold for £25,000 (her build cost has been estimated at £500,000) and converted into a cable-laying ship. She was bought by Thomas Brassey and Sir Daniel Gooch (who were later to become founding shareholders in Hughes' new company) and in 1864 / 1865 she laid the first transatlantic telegraph cable between Britain and the USA. Under the supervision of Gooch from 1866 to 1878 the ship laid over 26,000 miles of submarine telegraph cable in several parts of the world.

The Great Eastern was finally broken up for scrap on the River Mersey in North West England in 1889. A few years later, the newly formed Liverpool football club was looking for a flag pole for their ground and subsequently purchased the ship's top mast. It was erected alongside the newly constructed Kop terrace where it still stands today.

Many other famous ships of the time were built either at Millwall or the Thames ironworks including HMS Warrior, the Royal Navy's first ironclad warship, launched in 1860 at the Thames ironworks.

Charles Dickens in his 1861 novel Great Expectations provides an excellent contemporary picture of the London docks scene. He describes Pip's journey down the Thames with its *'tiers of shipping. Here, were the Leith, Aberdeen and Glasgow steamers, loading and unloading goods ... here, were colliers by the score and score ... here ... was tomorrow's steamer for Rotterdam ... and here tomorrow's for Hamburg ... again among the tiers of shipping ... hammers going in ship-builders yards.'*

But daily working life on the Isle of Dogs was somewhat less romantic; the place was full of factories and docks and was therefore very much a working class district with migrants from all over Britain. Much of the housing that had been built was the typical Victorian dwelling house, rented out to several occupants and they were ill adapted to meet the requirements of a working man's home. Although Londoners were used to living in rented rooms, many of the workers and their families had come from the provinces and were used to being in individual cottages. The living conditions caused much unpleasantness and ill feeling among the residents. After the 1866 London financial crash, several local companies were forced to close and many workers lost their jobs or were on short time and this led to considerable poverty and hardship. It is impossible to say how much of all this was noticed by Hughes during his time at Millwall but he must have been aware of the social problems in his daily contact with his own workers. But it hardly seems coincidental that during his time in Russia he was so concerned about the welfare of his workers, especially the issue of housing. Another interesting pointer to the future approach of Hughes in Russia is the fact that there was very little in the way of amusement or entertainment in the area around Millwall. But during the 1860s in the winter months, the Millwall ironworks organised periodic lectures in the company dining-hall and these proved popular and were generally well attended.

As a director of the Millwall ironworks, Hughes must have been paid a handsome salary. Despite having to provide for a large family, he was able to afford a house in Greenwich and amass considerable savings, as we shall see later when we look at the formation of his new company. Greenwich was a smart London suburb directly across the River Thames from Millwall and the Hughes' home was close to the Royal Naval College there. The 1860s were a momentous time for the British Royal Navy. As sail was giving way to steam, it had taken the decision to modernise its fleet of famous wooden 'men of war'. Armaments technology was advancing; bigger cannon with improved range were becoming available. Stronger ships were needed both to carry these heavier guns and to survive their bombardment. The answer lay with the new iron clad warships and the Royal Navy decided to conduct a series of trials to find the best system of iron plating.

The trials, which were held at various dockyards, were relatively rudimentary and consisted of using very old wooden warships equipped with armour plating from various British and French manufacturers. Millwall ironworks was well known by then for the quality of its iron as well as the technical genius of Hughes and the company was invited to participate. During his period at Millwall, he had invented a new method for mounting heavy naval guns which was used on many war ships of the time. Known eponymously as the 'Hughes Stringer', this invention would have meant Hughes was already very familiar to the British navy.

From the trials held in Portsmouth in March 1864, the Royal Navy concluded that the Millwall iron plates were superior to any of the others tested. As a result, the reputation of Millwall and Hughes soared and brought him to the attention of many other navies who were simultaneously going through the same re-armament process. The success in the British navy trials led to his first known direct contact with the imperial Russian government. But it was not iron plating for ships that initially interested

18

the Russians, it was Hughes' expertise in iron cladding for their strategically important naval fortress at Kronstadt in the Baltic that they were in the process of reinforcing.

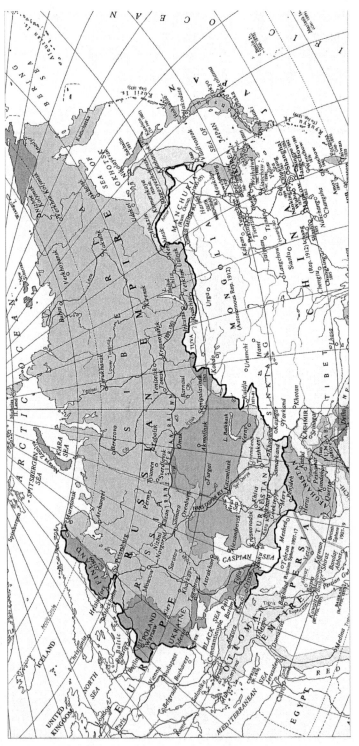

Map of Tsarist Russia in the late 19th century
(reproduced with kind permission of Philips)

CHAPTER TWO

Crimean War, Kronstadt and Ukraine

John Hughes' initial dealings with the Russian government came as a direct result of the consequences of the Crimean War that had taken place a few years earlier. His subsequent involvement in Ukraine and the founding of Hughesovka also followed from the strategic implications for the Russian government of this war. Although known as the Crimean War, it was actually fought on two fronts – in the Crimean part of the Ukraine and the Baltic campaign around Kronstadt in the Gulf of Finland. Russia's defeat in this war was to have major impacts on the future development of the country both industrially and socially. When hostilities broke out in 1853, initially with the Turkish Empire, later joined by the French and British, Russia was ill-equipped to fight a major war. It had fallen behind in the technological and social changes that emanated from the Industrial Revolution and the resultant impacts on military capabilities and logistical support. Despite having a relatively large army, Russia's armaments largely dated from the Napoleonic War 40 years earlier. It had no railways south of Moscow and was forced to supply its Crimean forces in the Ukraine by ox-carts.

The Crimean campaign began in earnest when a joint invasion force, over 60,000 strong, comprising British, French and Turkish troops landed in Calamita Bay, in the southern Crimea on September 14th 1854. A few days later, the three armies marched south along the coast towards Sebastopol, 30 miles away. In their path lay the river Alma and on the heights to the south of the river, the Russian general Prince Menschikoff had prepared his defences. He boasted that his troops would be able to hold their positions for at least three weeks and the ladies of Sebastopol travelled to the Alma to enjoy both a picnic and the spectacle of the repulse of the invaders.

On September 20th the allies, under the joint commands of General Lord Raglan, Marshal St Arnaud and General Omar Pasha, moving westwards, reached the Alma and engaged the Russians in battle. The French were tasked with turning the left (or seaward) flank of the defenders, at which point the British were to make a frontal assault (across a stream and then uphill in the face of withering fire from Russian infantry and artillery). Due to the first of a catalogue of misunderstandings and misapprehensions which characterised this war, the British attacked before the French had achieved their objective, with consequent heavy casualties. Lord Raglan (who was fighting his first battle since Waterloo, when he had been on the staff of the Duke of Wellington) moved so far in advance of his troops that he was actually directing the battle from behind the Russian front line. However, after some three hours, the Russians were completely routed and fled from the field in undisciplined retreat. Lord Raglan wished to pursue the fleeing Russians, but the French under Marshal St Arnaud, refused. As a result, the Russian army retook Sebastopol and a clever young military engineer, Lieutenant Colonel Todleben (who we will meet again later), began to prepare the town's defences. The Allied armies, deciding not to attack Sebastopol from the north, marched southeast towards Balaklava harbour which was captured without bloodshed and became the British supply base. Siege weapons and ammunition could now be landed and the allies opened up their bombardment of Sebastopol on October 17th 1854, and continued it for the next two days without out noticeable success.

On October 25ᵗʰ 1854, Menschikoff made a major assault on the right of the besieging armies, whose forward defences were a few improvised gun emplacements manned by Turkish militia. Although the Turks fought bravely for over two hours, they were driven back and the fleeing Turks regrouped on either side of four companies of the 93ʳᵈ Highlanders under Sir Colin Campbell, which were the only troops between the advancing Russians and the British base at Balaklava. Shortly afterwards a further two companies of the Highlanders, and a rag-tag of men from the port (including invalids from the hospital) joined this last line of defence. These men came under Russian artillery fire and a strong force of Russian cavalry moved in their direction. Campbell formed his men into line (not a square, which was the accepted way for infantry to face a cavalry charge) and the Russian advance was driven off with volleys of musket fire. This action became known as 'the thin red line' from the report filed by The Times correspondent W. H. Russell in which he used the phrase *'a thin red streak, tipped with a line of steel'*. Whilst these actions were taking place, the Russians were calmly removing the British guns from the Causeway Heights which had been abandoned by the Turks. Lord Raglan ordered his Light Cavalry Brigade and his infantry into action to prevent this and the famous Charge of the Light Brigade began but sadly in completely the wrong direction. Over 650 men charged forward and well over a hundred of them died within the next few minutes. As the Light Brigade went in, Raglan's infantry finally arrived on the battlefield but their only success was the recapture of the westernmost redoubts on the Causeway Heights. By the end of this chaotic day, the British had lost possession of a considerable amount of ground, including the majority of their forward defences, as well as the only metalled road in the area.

The Russians attacked the British a few days later in what became the battle of Inkermann. There was little decisive leadership shown on either side but after a day of heavy fighting in thick fog, the British found themselves holding the field (having received useful, if belated, help from the French). The Russian casualties exceeded the numbers of Allied troops that had been attacked and in total, over 17,500 men (mostly Russian infantry) were killed or wounded. After the Battle of Inkermann, the weather deteriorated to such an extent that no further serious action was possible and the allies were restricted to siege operations. The winter of 1854 / 55 revealed serious shortcomings in the British military supply system as thousands of men died from illness, exposure and malnutrition – four times as many died from disease as did from enemy action (see also comments about Thomas Brassey on page 41). In June 1855 an assault began on the outer defences of Sebastopol on the anniversary of the Battle of Waterloo. These initial attacks failed but on September 8th 1855 the allies again stormed Sebastopol, this time successfully and the Russians evacuated the town. With the fall of Sebastopol, the war in the Crimea effectively came to an end, although hostilities were not fully suspended until February 1856 with peace declared at the end of March.

Russia's failure in the Crimean War proved to be an important watershed in the future development and modernisation of the country. The defeat had three major impacts. It caused political unrest, especially among the peasants due to conscription into the militia during the war, contributing to the decision to emancipate serfs in 1861. It caused severe financial problems – the Russian government was left with a debt burden of one billion roubles and it exposed the backwardness of the country's economy and its outdated military capabilities. The new Tsar Alexander II and his government took on board the lessons of defeat and steadily moved to tackle these three issues. In doing so, the results of their actions were to prove vital in paving the way for the arrival of John Hughes. The emancipation of the serfs led to a gradual improvement in labour mobility and flexibility, essential for industrialisation. Under von Reutern, the new minister of finance, taxation, accounting and the public finances were overhauled and modernised and a state bank was founded in 1860. Lastly, Alexander's government decided to aggressively follow a policy of industrialisation, particularly expanding the railway network, coal and metallurgical manufacturing due to their strategic importance.

Kronstadt was founded by Peter the Great, who captured the island of Kotlin in the Gulf of Finland from the Swedes in 1703. The first fortifications were inaugurated there in 1704, chiefly as a protection for the Russian capital at that time, Saint Petersburg. The Gulf waters are not very deep in this area, so during the winter it completely freezes over. Workers constructed thousands of frames of oak logs filled with stones which were carried by horses across the frozen sea and placed in holes cut into the ice. Thus, several new small islands were created and forts were erected on them, effectively closing all access to St Petersburg by the sea. Only two narrow navigable channels remained, and the strongest forts guarded them.

Kronstadt was then thoroughly refortified in the 19th century (with considerable help from two British engineers, Baird and Gascoigne – see page 175) and successfully defied the Anglo-French fleets during the Baltic campaign of the Crimean war. This campaign essentially remained a backwater in the conduct of the war as the main land battles took place in the Crimea and overshadowed the significance of this theatre. From the beginning, the Baltic campaign turned into a stalemate. The outnumbered Russian Baltic fleet confined its movements to the areas around its coastal fortifications. The British and French commanders – although they led the largest fleet assembled since the Napoleonic wars – considered Russian fortifications, especially the Kronstadt fortress, too well-defended to engage and limited their actions to blockading Russian trade and conducting raids on less fortified sections of the Finnish coast. Russia was dependent on imports for both the domestic economy and the supply of her military forces and the blockade seriously undermined the Russian economy and its ability to sustain the war.

Although Kronstadt successfully protected St Petersburg, the government recognised that further improvements would be needed to withstand the increasing firepower of modern fighting ships and so a new fort and batteries were commissioned to defend the principal approach to the capital. Following peace with Britain and France, work started on these in 1856 under the direction of General Todleben (who had been in charge of the Sebastopol fortifications in the Crimean War and subsequently promoted). He visited England later that year to look at new armaments and may well have met Hughes at Millwall to discuss armour plating on this trip. Construction continued sporadically for the next 15 years and Emmanuel Nobel (of the famous Swedish Noble family) developed and built mine barriers for Kronstadt and founded a local metalworking and engineering plant. By this time, the state of the art for such fortifications was to armour them with thick iron plates. Lacking the capability to do this domestically, the Russians cast around for a foreign company that could carry out such improvements at Kronstadt.

In 1921 a group of sailors and soldiers in Kronstadt together with some civilian supporters rebelled against the Bolshevik regime. Their demands included freedom of speech, a stop to the deportation to concentration camps, a change of Soviet war politics and liberation of the soviets (workers' councils) from Party control. After brief negotiations Leon Trotsky, then the Minister for War in the Soviet government, responded by sending troops to Kronstadt and the uprising was ruthlessly suppressed. This was the last major revolt against Communist rule within Russia proper until the dissolution of the Soviet Union in 1991.

The reputation of the Millwall ironworks and John Hughes' considerable experience in this technology had by now reached the notice of the Russian government. In 1864 an order was duly placed with Millwall and General Todleben, accompanied by another Russian army engineer Colonel Guern, came to London to liaise on production at the works. Todleben was by now an aide de camp to the Tsar and so well placed to represent Russia's interests. It was they who in discussions with Hughes first raised the problem of railway building and industrialisation in Russia. At this time there were less than 1000 miles of railroad in the country and the government was anxious to expand its network quickly for both strategic and economic reasons. But it also recognised that it was heavily dependent on the large quantities of iron rails currently being imported, much of it from South Wales with the works at Dowlais, Cyfarthfa and Ebbw Vale being the main suppliers. Russia's domestic iron industry remained antiquated, mostly still using charcoal furnaces with the majority of production coming from the Urals, relatively remote from the primary area of desired initial rail expansion in the west and south of Russia. The government realised that from both a strategic and economic viewpoint building a railway network would require large, modern iron producing facilities within Russia and the Ukraine was potentially an ideal place to do this.

The two Russians apparently also outlined to Hughes the interest of their government in attracting foreign capital and expertise to develop the significant coal and iron resources known to exist in the Ukraine region. The Russian officials probably couldn't believe in their good luck. Having come to England to supervise the purchase of armaments, they now found themselves as EG Bowen[4] puts it in his biography of Hughes, *face to face with ... a man of vast experience in the very work of manufacturing iron rails* (who had) *worked at the world's chief producing centres*! Whether this was destiny or serendipity, the coincidence of capabilities and interests was too great for either party

---

4   EG Bowen – John Hughes (Hughesovka), 1978

to ignore. As a result of these discussions, Hughes was invited to go to Russia to look for himself. Although the timing is uncertain, this was probably in 1867, following completion of the fortification work at Kronstadt.

It seems various opportunities within Russia were discussed with Hughes during this visit, including managing the large government iron foundry at Kolpino near St Petersburg. [5] After visiting the Kolpino site, Hughes concluded that it needed too much modernisation and was not right for him. He was more interested in the green field possibilities offered by southern Russia. The Russian government had been well aware of the enormous potential of the Donbass for many years but the riches of the region had so far only been slowly developed by a few Russian and foreign entrepreneurs. The Russians had previously been much more interested in expanding production in their preferred Urals region, despite its lack of coal and difficulties in moving iron west to the main markets. Coal had been mined in the Donbass on a limited scale for several decades but production failed to expand due to lack of technical expertise and investment capital. The government had set up an ironworks in Lugansk (see page 61) to take advantage of the local coal and using iron from the Urals. But this proved to be economically unviable as a long-term operation. It was not until the mid-1860s that the existence of workable local iron deposits was discovered following several detailed geological surveys. The government then tried again with a works in Lisichansk using local coal and iron but this also failed.

So in 1866, the government tried a new approach, granting

---

5   Kolpino was established by the Russian admiralty in the mid-18th century and had strong British connections, having been run by Charles Gascoigne and then William Alexander, both of whom had distinguished careers in Russia. It was the latter's recent retirement that prompted the Russians to seek Hughes as a replacement.

concessions in the area to several Russian and British entrepreneurs but none of these had been fully exploited. One of the Russian concession holders was a Prince Serge Kochubei, who in 1868 had been granted the rights for a rail manufacturing works but had been unable to raise the necessary funds to pursue his concession. During Hughes' trip to St Petersburg, the Grand Duke Constantin, the younger brother of Alexander II, met Hughes, advising him of Prince Kochubei's situation and suggested that he should establish a company to purchase this concession and develop the extensive coal and iron deposits in the Donbass. The Duke had been in charge of the Russian navy until 1865 and probably knew Hughes from his recent work at Kronstadt. Coincidentally, a favourable report on the Donbass coal and iron potential had recently been completed for the Duke by two English engineers, Swan and Hume. They had looked in detail at the Ekaterinoslav region, especially the estates of a Prince Paul Lieven around the river Kalmius which contained large coal deposits. A copy of this report was given to Hughes and he set off to tour the region, accompanied by Hume and Alexander Cameron (a Scottish friend of his who was then working in Russia and who later joined his company). A knowledgeable local Ukrainian guide was provided and Hughes visited the area, evaluating the possibilities and was very impressed with what he saw. Hughes recognised the enormous opportunity offered by the Donbass region and as a result of this visit, immediately started to formulate his initial plans for the future. Indeed, whilst with Hume in Ekaterinoslav, Hughes *laid out the whole plan of the future works, and gave* (Hume) *instructions for the erection of wooden buildings to accommodate the workmen*. [6]

George Hume was an engineer who had been living in Russia for the past ten years. Born in London in 1836, he was now based in Kharkov and knew the Ukraine well. He was a leading importer of English agricultural equipment and had been involved in set-

---

6   George Hume – Thirty-Five Years in Russia, 1914

ting up several companies in Russia. He formed a relationship with Hughes that was to last for many years and as a Russian speaker no doubt helped him with local negotiations in the early days as well as general advice on doing business in Russia. The connection with Hughes was further strengthened soon after by a chance meeting while Hume was travelling in the Donbass in 1868. He met engineers constructing the Kharkov to Azov railway line and among them was William Gooch, nephew of Sir Daniel Gooch, chairman of the British Great Western Railway. William Gooch was looking for business opportunities in Russia and after discussing various possibilities, Hume and Gooch decided to go into business together, setting up a steam powered flour mill, with the latter becoming the resident manager. The £21,000 investment needed for the new mill was provided by William's father John Gooch. The latter was at this time working with Hughes to promote the new Russian venture and John Gooch was to become a major investor in his company, along with his son Charles and his brother Sir Daniel Gooch. It is not clear whether or not Hume actually followed up the instructions from Hughes to start initial construction work. However, most modern Ukrainian sources give 1869 as the date for the founding of Hughesovka, not 1870 as in all English references. Also in a later listing of Welsh workers at Hughes' company a William Thomas is shown as having joined in 1869, prior to the arrival of Hughes in Ukraine in 1870 to start building the works. This is unlikely to be an error in the company's records. It also seems unlikely that Hughes, who was a meticulous planner, would have arrived off the Black Sea coast with all his ships and men without some kind of proemial organisation. So it is probable that an advance party was sent out to Ukraine to work with Hume on initial logistics and preparing the chosen site.

On his return to England, no doubt imbued with enthusiasm and his head buzzing with ideas, Hughes began the work of setting up a new company and finding investors. In London, he discussed his ideas with friends and business associates and was quickly able to

30

generate sufficient initial interest in raising the capital needed to set up the operation in Ukraine. This was no mean achievement given the tensions and cool diplomatic relations between Britain and Russia at the time as a result of the Crimean War. The positive report by Swan and Hume on the region's potential that had been given to Hughes during his recent visit would have been an important factor in helping him subsequently raise the necessary finance. With the potential investment secured, Hughes returned to St Petersburg and entered into a series of extremely complex negotiations. First he had to negotiate with Prince Lieven for the various mining and land rights required for the new company and once this was done, Hughes could discuss suitable terms with Prince Kochubei for his concession rights. He then had to obtain approval of the Russian government for these terms and finally last but not least, Hughes had to keep his potential British investors on side with the twists and turns of all these negotiations. It seems the Prince was glad to transfer his concession to Hughes as the Prince felt the terms were quite favourable to him. As the Lievens were also friends of the Kochubei family this no doubt helped with progressing the negotiations. Like Prince Kochubei, Prince Lieven was a member of one of Russia's leading aristocratic families and was a major landowner in the Donbass region. His uncle had been appointed the Tsar's minister plenipotentiary to the Court of St James's in London in 1814, a post which he held for 22 years and his cousin Prince Alexander Lieven had been governor of the Black Sea port of Taganrog, the port later used by Hughes for importing his equipment.

Given the potential pitfalls when such negotiations take place between people from two very different cultures and languages, Hughes did remarkably well to finalise all this within a few months. He concluded a deal with Prince Lieven on December 18th 1868 for the rights to work the coal and iron deposits on his land, the lease of land necessary to construct a rail link to the new works plus the right to purchase an additional quantity of land as necessary in the future. After his initial discussions with Prince Kochubei, Hughes was so confident about the business potential that he approached the government with a request to expand the original concession to include a locomotive works and the rights to extensive railway building but these were refused by the government.

A deal was finally struck between Hughes and Prince Kochubei and this was formally approved by the Russian minister of railways on April 15th 1869 and published by the government just three days later. Apparently, the Tsar became interested in this British entrepreneur and once the details of the agreement were finalised, Hughes reportedly met Tsar Alexander II in the Winter Palace[7]. Comprehensive Articles of Agreement were then drawn up in Russian and English representing all parties involved and signed in London on May 28th 1869. The contents of these Articles are somewhat complex (they ran to ten foolscap pages of closely written copperplate handwriting) but essentially they provided the following rights and obligations –

Hughes undertook to form an English company to construct an iron smelting works and rail plant, mine coal and to build an 85 kilometre rail link from his works to the main Kharkov – Azov line, then currently under construction. The blast furnace had to be operational within nine months and capable of producing 100 tonnes of cast iron per week and 2,000 tonnes of coal per day had to be available for shipment once the new rail link was operational. These were very demanding commitments for a start-up green field operation in such an underdeveloped part of Russia and were to cause Hughes great anxiety in the months ahead. However, in return, at the end of ten years Hughes' new company was to receive all the land initially leased plus any additional land

---

7 George Hume – ibid

that may have been rented locally meanwhile for expansion of the works. Also the company would receive a government subsidy of 50 kopecks per pud (approximately 30 roubles per tonne) for rails supplied for Russian railways over the next ten years. This was a substantial incentive for Hughes as the initial price agreed with the government for rails was 1.38 roubles per pud. It's worth noting that this same level of subsidy had already been on offer from the government for several years but not successfully taken up by any other entrepreneurs. The fact that Hughes (together with his backers) was willing to take on the risks is an indication of his determination, commercial acumen and detailed planning abilities. As negotiations progressed, he realised there was one further important element to be resolved. The Russian government's current approach to tariffs was to reduce duties on most imported coal and iron and increase them on machinery and equipment. This was largely to encourage Russian industry to stand more on its own feet and partly to improve relationships with Britain. Hughes now discovered that most of the items he would need to import to build the works were covered by high tariffs while the products of his company would be largely competing in a duty free market. He managed to obtain agreement that all the construction materials and equipment needed for the project could be imported duty free. This was an important concession that Hughes obtained and meant that with the production subsidy, he would be well placed to successfully compete in the Russian market.

The land rights incorporated in the concession included both Crown lands with iron and coal deposits, as well as those of Prince Lieven. As part of the deal, George Fronstein, a well established St Petersburg merchant was given the rights to market rails from the works for seven years. Hughes also undertook to employ and train Russian workers in all but the very senior roles in the company. Although the final agreement was clearly ambitious in its scope and terms, one has to admire the breathtakingly comprehensive scope of what Hughes negotiated. He had the rights to large tracts of land containing iron and coal, adjacent supplies of water and lime for the manufacturing process. The lime came from the nearby village of Elenovka, which was later connected by rail to Hughesovka. Hughes also had price guarantees and production subsidies, duty free import rights for equipment, the right to build a vital rail link, marketing arrangements, financial backing and support from key Russian officials. The only significant foreseeable weakness in his plans was the lack of workers, skilled or otherwise at the chosen location. This was to prove an important issue for Hughes for many years as we shall see.

Hughes now moved rapidly to consolidate his plans. He paid Kochubei for his concession with £24,000 in shares in the new company plus 30,000 silver roubles. He agreed to lease (later buying) some 7,500 acres of land in his chosen area of operation from Prince Paul Lieven. The Prince was given an option for 400 shares in the new company by Hughes and was to remain involved in supporting the business for many years. Within a few months the arrangements were complete and on June 18th 1869, The Times published confirmation of his concession and the formation of the company. The choice of name – the New Russia Company – seems simple and straightforward but it may have had other resonances in Hughes' mind. The Ukraine at the time was known within the Tsarist Empire as 'Little' or the 'New Russia' and there had already been a previous 'Russia Company' founded by the English Merchant Adventurers in 1555. We don't know for certain whether Hughes was aware of these facts but it seems likely this choice of company name was not entirely coincidental. His choice was also a little unusual in the sense that most companies established in Russia traditionally incorporated in their name the locality in which they operated. But as Hughesovka did not yet exist, it would have been difficult for Hughes to follow local practice!

The first Russia Company dates from the age of Queen Elizabeth I and the early Stuarts when the chartered company, in the modern sense of the term, had its rise. The history of the original Russia Company begins in 1553, when a group of around 240 Londoners financed an expedition to discover the northeast passage to Cathay (modern China). The expedition had mixed motives. It hoped to copy the success of the Spanish and Portuguese in discovering new riches and products that could be brought back for sale in Britain. There was also the hope of discovering new markets for the export of English cloth, a trade then in decline, plus a potential northeast passage was important because it would be free of Portuguese interference. Sadly, the voyage failed in its original purpose, for the crews of two of the three ships froze to death during the northern winter. However the third ship, the *Edward Bonaventure*, under the command of Richard Chancellor, found safe anchorage in the mouth of the Dvina. Chancellor was then invited to Moscow, where Tsar Ivan IV agreed to allow English merchants to come and trade. The voyage thus led to the very first direct trade with Russia. In 1555 this enterprise was incorporated by royal charter as a joint stock company as the '*marchants adventurers of England, for the discovery of lands, territories, iles, dominions, and seigniories unknowen*' and it quickly became known as the Russia Company. The company's monopoly of English trade with Russia included the rights to trade without paying customs duties or tolls and to trade in the interior. The principal imports from Russia were furs, tallow, wax, timber, flax, tar and hemp and the main export to Russia was English cloth. The Russia Company also carried on a large trade with Persia through Russian territory; but this business gradually declined from various causes.

The Company in London appointed agents or 'factors' in Russia, hence the term 'British Factory' for the group of British agents. The original headquarters of the factory was in Moscow but in 1723 they moved by Imperial decree to the new capital St Petersburg. With the expansion of trade in the 19th century, the number of trading posts maintained by the company grew to include Archangel, Kronstadt, Moscow and St Petersburg. By the end of the 18th century there were around 1000 British residents in

St Petersburg with another much smaller community remaining in Moscow. During the 19th century, the impact and influence of the British in Russia grew steadily. There was an increasing admiration among the upper classes for the British way of life, its institutions and literature. The British traders provided a wide range of goods that became indispensable to the Russian elite – books, furniture, clocks, clothing, beer, medicine, horses, carriages and even gardeners. Several English shops were established in St Petersburg and many of the more prosperous merchants built homes along what was now called 'the English Embankment'. Since 1917 the Russia Company has operated principally as a charity and has given grants to English chaplaincies working within Russia.

New Russia Company share certificate

CHAPTER THREE
Setting up the Company, Works and Town

Hughes' new company was registered in London as company number 4467 on July 3rd 1869 with a nominal share capital of £300,000 (over £28 million today) divided into 6,000 shares of £50 each – clearly a very large sum. Hughes had worked fast since his return from Russia to set up the company so quickly and had persuaded some of his successful contemporary entrepreneurs to invest in the new venture. However, it would have been logical for Hughes to have canvassed possible investors prior to visiting Russia to conclude the agreement with the government. He was clearly now well connected in London as the list of shareholders reads almost like a who's who of famous Victorian entrepreneurs and included three baronets plus a member of parliament – Sir Daniel Gooch, his brother John Gooch, Thomas Brassey, his son Lord Brassey and Sir Joseph Whitworth. In addition four Russians acquired shares. There were 19 holders of the ordinary 'A' shares at the outset, including –

Sir Daniel Gooch MP	100
Charles Gooch	100
Thomas Brassey	200
Lord Thomas Brassey	50

Alexander Ogilvie	100
Sir William Wiseman	40
Sir Joseph Whitworth	100
Robert Peel	10
Robert Neale	10
William Woodgates	10
Prince Paul Lieven	400
Samuel Gruyen	100
Major General Ottomar Guern	100
Count Dmitry Nesselrode	40
Theodore Aston	40
Henry Alexander	20
Brinsley de Courcy Nixon	20

Three other people held a further 12 'A' shares between them, giving a total of only 1452 shares actually issued initially out of the authorised 6000. However, not even all these shares were paid for as the company had only received some £40,000 in payment by the end of 1869. Most, if not all the Russians were given their shares as part of the original deal struck by Hughes in Russia. This was not only in recognition of services already rendered but clearly there was an expectation on his part of continuing future support for the company. The company also issued 1000 'B' shares split equally between John Hughes and John Gooch, raising a further £50,000. Thus the initial share issue raised a total of £90,000 of which £25,000 (worth £2.4 million today) was from Hughes himself. This investment by Hughes provides a measure of his own financial position at the time as well as signalling his personal commitment to the eventual success of the new company. From the initial share subscription funds, Hughes had also to deposit £20,000 in a Russian bank as a performance bond guaranteeing his commitments to the government so the actual cash available at the very start was not as high as some sources have indicated.

A brief look at the backgrounds of some of these investors shows the kind of contacts Hughes now had and the circles in which he moved. Of course they invested in the hope of making good profits but they would have known from the outset that the New Russia Company was not a get-rich-quick venture. This was a high risk capital intensive project that would require some years to make a return. The fact that they did invest was largely due to their confidence in Hughes and his ability to manage the business. Reading through these brief histories, it is also interesting to see the various links with both Hughes' previous business interests as well as his ambitions for the new company. Hughes brought on board as shareholders some of the best connected people in Britain and Russia with between them knowledge of railways, engineering, manufacturing, armaments, banking, the Royal Navy plus the Russian Court and military establishment.

Sir Daniel Gooch was born on August 24th 1816 at Bedlington, Northumberland. He was trained as a railway engineer and moved on at an early age to locomotive construction. Isambard Kingdom Brunel, the engineer of the Great Western Railway (GWR), recognised Gooch's talents and chose him as the company's first locomotive superintendent. He joined the GWR one week before his 21st birthday and became Brunel's closest supporter and friend. Gooch was one of the outstanding locomotive engineers of the period, designing the best locomotives of the time. His engines set records for speed and safety not previously deemed possible, achieving standards that were not exceeded in his lifetime. In 1860 he began a set of associations which used his talents in engineering, finance and organization to inaugurate telegraphic communication between Britain and the United States. As a member of the boards of the three interested companies – the Great Eastern Steamship Company, the Telegraph Constructions and Maintenance Company, and the Anglo-American Telegraph Company, Gooch was able to co-ordinate the entire enterprise. In 1865 he became chairman of the GWR and rescued it from bankruptcy. Gooch was rewarded with a baronetcy in November 1866 and he was also the Conservative MP for Cricklade from 1865 to 1885.

John Viret Gooch born in 1812, was the brother of Sir Daniel Gooch and like his brother was intimately involved in the development of railways in 19th century Britain. He held the position of locomotive superintendent of the London and South Western Railway (LSWR) from 1841 to 1850. Gooch also designed a number of locomotives for the LSWR.

Sir Joseph Whitworth originated from Stockport and at a young age developed an interest in machinery. He initially worked as a mechanic in Manchester and then moved to London where he helped with the manufacture of Charles Babbage's calculating machine. He returned to Manchester in 1833 to start his own business manufacturing lathes and other machine tools, which were renowned for their high standard of workmanship. In 1841 Whitworth devised a standard for screw threads and its adoption by the British railway companies led to its widespread acceptance in industries worldwide and it later became a British Standard. He later also became involved in armaments manufacturing, introducing various improvements to gun technology. At the Great Exhibition in London in 1851, among 13,000 exhibitors, Whitworth had the largest display of any competitor with 23 exhibits of lathes and metal working machines. At the end of the 19th century, his company was merged with its great rival William Armstrong to form the famous British engineering company, Armstrong Whitworth. Prior to his death in 1887, he set up a government trust with the sum of £128,000 (worth over £13 million today) with the intention of 'bringing science and industry closer together'. The trust is still in operation, administered by the Institution of Mechanical Engineers.

Thomas Brassey was born near Chester in North West England in 1805. He worked initially as a land surveyor and in this capacity he met George Stephenson who encouraged Brassey to move into the new world of railway construction. He was unsuccessful at first but soon obtained his first contract for a viaduct and ten miles of railway near Stafford and this was the start of a long career building railways worldwide. In 1841 Brassey obtained the contract to build the Paris & Le Havre Railway in France and during the next ten years Brassey's company was involved in several railway projects in mainland Europe. He returned to England in 1843 building various major railways across the UK. Brassey was also responsible for the Victoria Docks in London and the Grand Trunk Railway in Canada. All told, Brassey built more than 6,500 miles of railway, including more than 20% of the British network and over 50% of the railways in France. Brassey also played an important part in building a railway during the Crimean War to supply the British forces during the siege of Sevastopol. The Black Sea port of Sevastopol was held by the Russians and was besieged in September 1854 by the British and Allied forces. It was hoped that the siege would be short but with the coming of winter the conditions for the British troops were appalling. It was proving very difficult to transport clothing, food, medical supplies and weaponry to the front and a very high number of men died or were invalided out. When news of the problem arrived in Britain, Brassey, together with two colleagues, offered to build a railway *at cost* in order to transport the British supplies. They shipped out the equipment and materials for building the railway, which had been intended for other undertakings, together with an army of navvies to carry out the work. Despite severe winter conditions, the railway to the troops was completed in just seven weeks and Sevastopol was finally taken in September 1855.

Brassey had other ideas which were well ahead of his time. He tried to interest the governments of Britain and Europe in the idea of a tunnel under the English Channel but these attempts came to nothing. He also wanted to build a canal through the Isthmus of Darién (now the Isthmus of Panama) but again he was unsuccessful. His career in railways lasted for more than 20 years and at its peak, Brassey was employing on average some 80,000 people in many countries across four continents. Despite this he never had a permanent office or staff and dealt with all the correspondence himself as many of the details of his projects were held in his memory. He was what today we would call a workaholic. In 1868 he suffered a mild stroke but he continued with his work, leaving in April 1869 on an extensive tour of various European countries. He died in Hastings in 1870 following a second stroke, leaving an estate estimated at the time to be worth well over £3 million. His eldest son, Lord Brassey, became an MP and went on to be Lord of the Admiralty.

Alexander Ogilvie had considerable experience of Russia as the manager of the St Petersburg office of Thomson Bonar & Company, a British merchant house that had been trading with Russia since the 18th century.

Sir William Wiseman was a senior officer in the British navy with good connections to the Admiralty and therefore an important contact for Hughes, especially given his interest in armaments.

Brinsley de Courcey Nixon originating from Ireland, Nixon was a banker in London and probably helped Hughes with financial advice and possibly arranged a loan for the company in its difficult first few years. His son eventually married one of Hughes' granddaughters.

Major General Ottomar Guern was one of the two Russians that originally visited Hughes at Millwall to discuss the Kronstadt fortification work and seemingly had been promoted in the interim.

Count Dmitry Nesselrode was a member of a prominent Russian family with strong political connections in St Petersburg and Moscow.

In the company memorandum, a very broad range of objectives are set out including the manufacture of locomotives, rolling stock, railway equipment and rails; armour-plated ships, iron forts and shields; munitions, shells and other weapons of war; to work iron and coal mines and to carry on the businesses of iron and steel manufacturers plus acting as dealers in coal, iron and brick. Clearly from the outset, the intention was to combine Hughes' knowledge and experience with Ukrainian resources to develop a major manufacturing and trading enterprise. Government control of joint stock companies in Russia in the latter half of the 19th century was quite onerous – whether Russian or foreign. Official permission was required not only to incorporate but to make any major changes in company structure, such as changing its capital, issuing new bonds or moving into a different area of business. It was a time consuming and potentially expensive process to make such changes. This partly explains why Hughes set out a broad prospectus for his new company at its inception.

Having established his new company, the next priority for Hughes was to finalise his plans for the construction of the ironworks and the settlement for the workers that would be needed alongside. Then he could order all the necessary equipment in Britain, arrange for its delivery to the docks and organise transport to Russia. On his return home to England in the summer of 1869 Hughes immediately started to place orders for the long list of materials and equipment required to set up the new enterprise in Russia. Many of the items, such as boilers, would have been made to order, requiring long lead times from the manufacturers. The whole project needed meticulous planning; everything to construct and operate the ironworks and coal mines, sets of tools, winter and summer clothing, household goods, furniture, food and money – all would have to be shipped out. At least he knew that as part of his agreement, the government had agreed to waive duty on all his equipment.

The New Russia Company's first blast furnace 1872 *(GRO)*

The blast furnaces in 1888 *(GRO)*

The blast furnaces in the 1890s *(GRO)*

The rail rolling mill *(GRO)*

Ox and horse drawn carts at the brickworks *(GRO)*

Steam engines at the works in the 1880s *(GRO)*

British workers in the machine shed in the 1890s *(GRO)*

A group of Russian workers, including several young boys *(GRO)*

A bullock train hauling a boiler 1910 (*GRO*)

Russian workers' housing *(GRO)*

Russian houses among the slag heaps close to the rolling mill *(GRO)*

The only other immediate problem was to sort out where he would obtain the skilled workers he needed since it was now clear there were none to be hired in Ukraine. Hughes knew that the kind of skilled workers required would have to be recruited in Britain. Although there was a certain familiarity with Russia, especially in South Wales due to the historical trade links, Hughes found it difficult to hire the men he needed. The remoteness of Ukraine and its harsh climate proved to be major obstacles and for those willing to go overseas at the time the USA was proving much more attractive. However, Hughes got lucky as in 1869 there was the start of a severe downturn in the iron industry in Britain. Most of the British rail network had now been built and so demand for iron rails dropped dramatically. At the same time, world markets were increasingly turning to steel rails. Many workers in those companies that had failed to modernise and change over to steel, lost their jobs or were on short time and started to consider migration to other parts of Britain or overseas. Indeed, the Merthyr Guardian ran a story in March 1869 referring to the 'emigration mania' that was sweeping the town and estimated that over 1,000 men were likely to emigrate that spring. The downturn caused considerable distress in South Wales and in Yorkshire, the two main rail manufacturing centres and marked the beginning of a steady, irreversible decline in the fortunes of the industry in South Wales and Merthyr in particular. The opportunity offered by the New Russia Company now looked more attractive and Hughes was eventually able to recruit the core group of experienced men he needed. Although some men came because they needed work, others joined due to the reputation of Hughes and through a sense of adventure.

The months prior to departure must have been an exceptionally busy period for Hughes. Setting up a new company, ordering all the equipment and recruiting his workers would have entailed an enormous amount of work and a great deal of co-ordination. Without an office or employees, Hughes had to handle all this administration and organisation on his own – a major achievement under the circumstances. It would also have been an emotionally difficult time as he was leaving behind his wife and children. Although his eldest four sons would eventually join him in Russia, his wife, daughter and youngest son stayed on in the family home in Greenwich. What the understanding was between Hughes and his wife at the time of his departure is not known but she never did join him in Russia. Hughes would return to London occasionally in later years for both business and social reasons but this was to be the last time the family would all be together. In the late summer of 1870, having carefully checked all his preparations, Hughes left England for Ukraine with eight chartered ships. They were full not only with all the initial equipment necessary to establish the works and mines but also much of the skilled labour – a group of about a hundred ironworkers and miners mostly from South Wales, plus all their immediate day-to-day living requirements. Their route was down through the Bay of Biscay, across the Mediterranean then on into the Black Sea and the Sea of Azov. Hughes was around 55 years old when he sailed from England for his new life in Russia. He was moving from the centre of the world's largest empire to the outer reaches of an empire in the world's largest country.

By the time the ships arrived at the Russian port of Taganrog, it was autumn. Off-loading some of the large equipment was very difficult as the ships had to stand some way off the coast due to the shallow nature of the Azov Sea and this caused delays. Once ashore, the long overland journey of close to 100 miles across the steppe began. All the materials and equipment Hughes brought from Britain had to be hauled to the site by ox-train along largely unmade tracks, across streams and ravines, often without bridges. Then the autumn rains turned the tracks to thick mud and the going became increasingly slow for the heavily laden ox-carts. Some became totally stuck and were abandoned for the winter, not being recovered until the following spring. To further complicate matters, Hughes found that tolls had to be paid to local landowners for the right to haul his wagons across private land.

46

Although the mineral resources of the region were plentiful, the landscape that he would have viewed on this visit must have been daunting. This part of the steppe was desolate, poor, sparsely populated with little in the way of transport links to the outside world. There were a few isolated villages and the dwellings were mostly poorly constructed huts. As he surveyed the site, the enormity of the task that lay ahead of him would have weighed heavily on his mind. But Hughes was committed; he had guaranteed his full personal involvement in this project to the Russian government, he now had his shareholders to satisfy and his group of British workers to look after. The location chosen by Hughes for his works was near the small mining settlement of Alexandrovka, founded in 1779, which later became absorbed into Hughesovka. His first home in Russia was on the farm of a woman landowner called Smolyaninova, on the right bank of the river Kalmius, in the governorship of Ekaterinoslav, about 60 miles inland from the Black Sea coast. This original site soon turned out to be not entirely suitable and Hughes quickly realised that to secure the long-term future of his operation, he would need to control both banks of the river. He therefore acquired more land from local Cossacks for a new site on the river's left bank, thereby assuring his water supplies, additional mineral resources and space for his future town to grow. Hughes' alertness and quick decision making in acquiring this new site for his works proved to be a major early advantage for him. This was the very beginning of Hughesovka. Life was very hard for the small group, especially through their first winter, which proved to be particularly severe.

As it turned out, the land rented from Prince Lieven contained the finest seam of coking coal in the Donbass. The overall Donbass coalfield is extensive – some 300 miles across and 60 miles from north to south – with four different types of coal. On his initial visit to the region, Hughes possibly would not have been aware that the land in his concession contained the same type of bituminous coal that he was familiar with in South Wales. As in Merthyr, bituminous coal provides the high grade coking coal needed for quality iron production. But Hughes had some knowledge of geology and would have quickly established the type of coal available to him. Hughes was also aware that there were only limited supplies of iron ore in the immediate vicinity but he knew that there were more deposits within the region so he decided to keep his own deposits in reserve, preferring to buy from other sources right from the start. Until Hughes could build rail links to the works, this iron ore had to be hauled by ox-trains across the steppe in the same laborious way that his original equipment had been. The New Russia Company eventually kept its own bullocks – 2,500 of them – to do the haulage work during the initial years until its rail network was completed.

Hughes knew well that he had to secure long-term sources of iron ore and once nearby Krivoi Rog was developed, Hughes quickly bought up extensive land there and the company operated its own mines (see page 86). This careful planning by Hughes, securing for the company control over all the major elements of production was an important key to its long-term economic success. It provided security of supply, control over costs and made the company less reliant on the vagaries of the Russian transport systems. It also seems Hughes was a tough negotiator and bargained hard for every deal, whether it was with the state, princely landowners, local iron ore producers or peasants for passage rights. As an experienced businessman, he understood the value of both buying at the right price as well as keeping good relations with his suppliers. The cumulative effect of this approach is illustrated by an 1896 study of costs at the five largest ironworks in the Donbass that found the New Russia Company's raw materials were between 10% and 45% lower than its competitors.[8]

The initial tasks of the newly arrived small British group were to

8   Theodore Friedgut – Iusovka and Revolution, 1989

build a smithy and start construction of the first blast furnace. Almost equally as important was to start work on the vital new rail link to nearby Constantinovka, thus connecting the works to the newly completed Kharkov to Azov line. The group also had to start building accommodation for the new local work force – initially simple wooden barracks. Hughes reportedly slept in one of the boilers they had brought with them for several weeks. Trying to comprehend the operational planning and logistics that must have been required to achieve all this with just 100 men is almost overwhelming. Whilst Hughes had his skilled workers from Britain, finding any local labour to help with the construction tasks in the barren Donetsk steppes was not going to be easy. Of the few people living on the nearby steppe at that time, the majority were peasants, eking out a largely subsistence living in a few small villages. By the end of 1870, the total population on site was only 164, mostly from Britain.

Recruiting and then retaining a stable, skilled workforce in this part of Russia was to prove to be a major challenge for the New Russia Company over many years. The general shortage of workers and the difficulties of employing them was a problem faced by all industrialists that came to southern Russia and was one that continued well into the 20th century. The problems Hughes faced were three-fold. First the pool of available skilled managers and technicians in Russia in 1870 was extremely limited, largely due to the country's low level of industrial development and lack of training. In southern Ukraine, with virtually no industry, it was non-existent. Building and then operating a modern ironworks would mean that all skilled workers would have to come from abroad.

The second problem was the relatively sparse population of the Donbass Steppes and thus an absence of a readily employable labour force. The few larger centres of population were not adjacent to the main coal and iron deposits and the rural population was very much tied to the land. When Hughes arrived, the region had one of the lowest population densities in the whole of Tsarist Russia. In many parts of Russia, low soil fertility and a short growing season did not permit the production of enough grain to ensure a year-round food supply. Thus a large proportion of the Russian male population was employed in seasonal migrant labour – mining, lumbering, barge hauling and increasingly factory work. However, the low population density of the Donbass meant peasant land holdings were relatively large. They could be more self-sufficient and were less motivated to seek external additional income. Whilst it was possible to recruit a limited number of peasants initially, particularly for the mines, it again meant that the majority of workers would have to come from outside the immediate area. This was to apply equally to the people needed later to provide the commercial support structure for a growing town – shopkeepers, tradesmen, administrators, etc. There were some coal miners working the local seams but this activity was mostly seasonal, an addition to working their land, not as a primary wage-earning occupation. Attempts were made by Hughes to recruit some of these men on permanent contracts but Russian labour laws regarding employment were rigorous and enforced. Once signed, they could not be broken to allow a return to the land, temporary or permanent, so initially there were few takers. Despite a massive 300% growth in the region's population to 1914, the shortage of labour in the Donbass remained a problem as demand from new industrial development continued to outstrip the local supply.

The third problem was the fact that even when local peasants were persuaded to work in the mines or ironworks, they usually retained strong links to their land or village. Many returned for the spring and summer and saw their industrial employment as merely a supplement to what they could earn from the land. This resulted in a very seasonal and unreliable workforce – a fundamental problem for ironworks needing continuous working to pay for their high capital cost and meet demand.

How much Hughes was aware of each of these problems at the outset is unclear. He would have certainly been well aware of the skilled labour shortage from his knowledge of Russia and his initial visit, which is why he brought his own team with him from Britain. He would also possibly have been aware of the likelihood of seasonal migration by some workers as this had been the experience in the early years of Welsh industrialisation. If he did know of the other labour problems, he probably underestimated the difficulties he would experience. Although Hughes was prepared from the start to train his new workforce, he was frustrated at the early problems in recruiting and retaining local labour. Friedgut quotes a letter from Hughes to a government minister in which he confessed –

'When I commenced these works I set my mind upon training the Russian workmen (knowing at the time that it would cost much time and money) with a view to creating a colony of iron-workers who would be attached to the place, and the Directors in London quite approved my plan. To attain this was my pride and ambition and it is discouraging that the results have not been more satisfactory after twelve months' experience.' [9]

But being the man he was, Hughes steadily put in place solutions to improve the position. He realised that much of his future labour force would have to be attracted from villages well outside the immediate area and that the transition to a stable workforce would involve a substantial change in their way of life. His approach to the problem became the model that was to be followed later by most other successful foreign entrepreneurs.

Hughes and his team had to work fast. They were under pressure as the company's agreement with the government set ambitious

---

9   Theodore Friedgut – ibid

start dates for output from the works and mines as well as minimum production levels. Their progress was also being constantly monitored by a government appointed engineer who filed monthly reports, the first one having been completed as early as December 1870. Hughes also sent reports, letters and telegrams direct to von Reutern, the Russian minister of finance as well as other ministers to update them on progress and problems encountered. The first months in Russia were problematic. A particularly severe winter with heavy snowfalls caused delays, a cholera outbreak caused the loss of several British and Russian workmen and the combination of the harsh winter and disease resulted in many of the British workers returning home. However, by April 1871, the first iron had been smelted – a major achievement under the circumstances. But difficulties arose almost immediately. After just a few days, the furnace had to shut down due to technical problems relating to temperature control and charging of the furnace. There was nothing wrong with the local materials and such initial problems were not unheard of in Europe. However, it took several months to resolve the problems and complete the necessary repairs. After a test firing of the furnace in November 1871, it was restored to full production of pig iron in January 1872. The workforce by this time was a mixture of British and Russians who had come from distant towns like Smolensk and Tula; very few local Ukrainians were as yet willing to become factory workers. This must have been a particularly challenging and stressful time for Hughes and the British workers he had with him. Keeping the group focused and motivated, so far from home and in such a harsh climate would have tested any man. Some would have given up as several of the other foreign entrepreneurs that had come to Ukraine to exploit its riches already had. But Hughes was determined and persevered, keeping his key men with him while the problems were resolved. Indeed Hughes may have been an inspiration to another new iron works in Ukraine. The Pastukov brothers were trying to set up an operation at Sulinovka near Lugansk using local iron ore and anthracite for smelting and experienced frequent early technical difficulties. It is likely they would have abandoned the project if it weren't for the nearby example of Hughes' persistence in the face of his technical problems. There was certainly contact between the two entrepreneurs; it seems they exchanged advice and ideas and the Pastukovs may also have assisted Hughes with translation help in the early days.

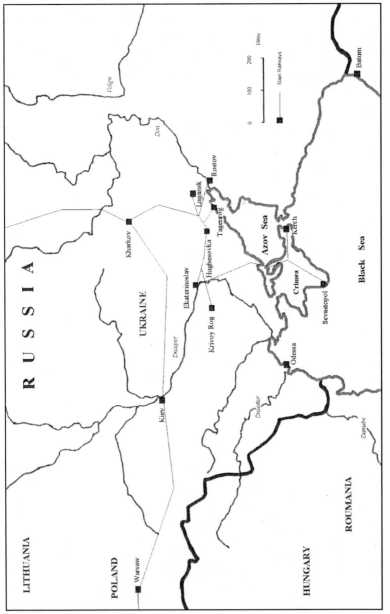

Map of southern Russia and Ukraine

CHAPTER FOUR
The Ukraine and Russian Industry

The Ukraine and southern Russia have a long history of being invaded and occupied by successive tribes and nationalities. After the Tatar-Mongolian invasions in the 13th century, much of the region remained largely uninhabited. To the north in Kiev and the west in Galicia, several independent principalities gradually became established and these in turn were later absorbed by Poland and Lithuania. The Ukrainian language and culture was largely suppressed and replaced by Polish and this oppression of the Ukrainian people by the Poles led to a series of insurrections. The Ukrainians sought protection from the Russians and following a prolonged war between Russia and Poland, a treaty was agreed splitting Ukraine along the Dnieper River. The lands on the western bank of the river remained under Polish control while those on the eastern bank were placed under the protection of the Russian Tsar. The partitions of Poland at the end of the 18th century placed most of the Ukrainian territory on the right bank of the Dnieper River under Russian rule and the Ukrainian peasants who had remained free were then enserfed. The westernmost part of Ukraine was incorporated into the Austrian Empire.

The south remained very much an under-populated frontier territory although Slavic people were pushing in from the east and these eventually became known as the Don Cossacks. By the 17th century the Crimean region and much of what later became known as the Donbass Steppes had been occupied by the Tatars who gradually came under Turkish rule. During the 18th century, the area came under increasing influence from the Germans to the west and the expanding Russian Empire to the north. The Russians moved further and further south, building small military forts as a line of defense against the Turks. After the Russian-Turkish war of 1768-1774, the Donbass was annexed to the Russian Empire, followed by the Crimea in 1783. Some measure of stability was now brought to the region and the population started to slowly grow with migrants from other parts of Ukraine, as well as smaller numbers from Russia, the Balkans plus Germany, and the southern lands came to be called New Russia. The area became a safe haven for many Ukrainian and Russian serfs and other fugitives from political, economic and religious subjugation and was ruled by the Cossacks. They were integrated into the Tsarist regime to become an important military force to control its new acquisition.

The linking of the right and left banks of the Dnieper and integration with southern Ukraine under the Russians in the 19th century provided for the first time a Ukrainian national and economic entity. This eventually gave rise to common interests that were occasionally to prove different from those of other parts of the Russian Empire. This resurgence of Ukrainian national consciousness fostered a renewed interest among intellectuals in Ukrainian history, culture, and language and the founding of many cultural and social societies. As before under the Poles, the Ukrainians now found themselves harassed by the Russian government. It responded to rising national feelings by harassing, imprisoning, and exiling leading Ukrainian intellectuals. Ukrainian academic and social societies were disbanded and publications, plays and concerts in Ukrainian were forbidden in 1876. Finally, the existence of a Ukrainian language and nationality was officially denied and the prohibition extended to education, a major contributing factor to the low rate of literacy among Ukrainians, which was only 13% at the end of the 19th century. Nevertheless, a Ukrainian national movement in the Russian Empire persisted, spurred partially by developments in western Ukraine, where Ukrainians in the more liberal Austrian Empire had far greater freedom to develop their culture and language.

When John Hughes and his group of British workers first arrived in Ukraine and travelled inland from the Black Sea coast, they entered a region that was relatively sparsely populated, despite its rich agricultural and mineral resources. Why was this? For generations, the southern Ukrainian steppe had been terrorised by slave traders. From the early 1500s until into the early 18th century, this area of Cossack grassy flatlands was the major source of slaves destined to meet the needs of the expanding Ottoman Empire. The Black Sea had become an 'Ottoman lake' and the trade was largely run by Tatars from the Crimea who were allied to the Ottomans. They carried out what became known as the 'annual harvesting of the steppe'. Arriving each year in strength and using large numbers of heavily armed men, the Tatars would scour the southern part of Ukraine, often sacking entire villages and towns. During this period, they carried off an estimated three million people – predominantly Ukrainians but also Russians, Belarusians and Poles into slavery. It has been estimated that about 15% of the population of Istanbul during this period consisted of slaves.

Although the horrors of the African slave trade are well documented, little attention has been given to the tragic trade in humans in this part of the world and the resulting economic and social impacts on the region. Contemporary Ukrainian culture has largely ignored the grim reality of this dreadful 'harvest' and the damage it caused. The only significant references relate to the celebrated story of the most famous of the Ukrainian slaves – Roxelana. She was enslaved in the mid-16th century and taken to Istanbul where she was sold, eventually becoming the wife of Suleyman the

Magnificent of the Ottoman Empire. She bore Suleyman five children and, in an astonishing break with tradition, was finally freed and became his only legal wife. This strengthened her position in the palace and eventually led to one of her sons, Selim, inheriting the empire. It appears that Roxelana may have acted as Suleyman's adviser on matters of state, and she seems to have had an influence upon foreign affairs and international politics. Two of her letters to the Polish King Sigismund II Augustus have been preserved. Some historians also believe that she may have intervened with her husband to control Crimean Tatar slave raiding in her native land. She died in 1558.

At a time when new nation states were emerging all across the fragmented map of medieval Europe, the Cossacks centred in Kiev, found it impossible to impose a centralised control over southern Ukraine due to the de-stabilising activities of the Tatars. But by depopulating the southern steppes, the Tatars unintentionally laid the region open to Russian colonisation, allowing the new imperial rulers to portray their conquest as virgin land for the taking. Neither the Crimean Tatars nor the Cossacks achieved the freedom they had struggled for, now finding themselves part of the Russian Empire. Although the slave trade was gradually largely suppressed by the Russians as they tightened their grip on the area, it didn't lead to any significant growth in population, at least inland on the steppes. The Russian expansion was initially mostly limited to the Ukrainian coast, largely for strategic reasons in their struggle with the Ottoman Empire. New Russian city colonies were founded around the Black Sea coastal stretch and they were given Greek-sounding names such as Mariupol and Melitopol to add a sense of imperial past and break with any local Cossack associations. Interestingly, these new lands became known as 'New Russia' a term echoed in the name chosen for John Hughes' company. As the struggle for power and influence continued between Russia, France, Turkey and Britain in the 19th century, the Ukrainian Black Sea hinterland remained largely undeveloped. The Russian strategic focus remained on expanding control of the Black Sea and developing trade through its newly acquired ports. In terms of its population density, southern Ukraine did not fully recover from this raiding until the late 19th century as the industrialisation process started by Hughes gathered pace and attracted new immigrants.

By the time of Hughes' arrival in Ukraine, it accounted for 18% of the Russian Empire's plants, 15% of its workers and 12% of the value of its output. Industrial activity was concentrated in the north around Kiev and Kharkov, with various consumer goods industries, sugar refineries and distilleries being the most developed and accounting for approximately 60% of Ukraine's output and number of workers. Recent improvements to transport had stimulated agricultural production and grain exports, especially to Britain, were increasingly important. The existence of large coal deposits in the Donbass region, along the Kalmius river, had been known to the Russians since the time of Peter the Great. On his way back to St Petersburg from the Azov crusade in 1696 he was told of the 'inflammable stone' and is reputed to have said, *'This mineral will be useful if not for us then for our descendants.'* However, exploitation did not really begin until the early 19th century to supply the newly opened Lugansk iron works and it remained small scale until the arrival of John Hughes in 1870, largely due to the lack of transportation and sparse local population. The industrialisation of the Donbass started by Hughes initiated a wave of migration in the latter part of the 19th century. As a whole, Ukrainians showed much less enthusiasm for migration to the new Donbas mining settlements and factory towns with only around a third of new settlers coming from the neighbouring Ukrainian regions. However, the Donbass proved an attractive destination for people from the Russian provinces of Kursk, Orel, Voronezh, Tula, Smolensk, Samara and Belorussia as well Greeks and Tatars from the Crimea, Croats from the Austrian-Hungarian Empire, Serbs and Bulgarians from the Ottoman Empire, Germans, Austrians,

Poles, and Jews. Out of this mix of ethnic backgrounds, the emerging working class in the Donbas developed into largely Russified urban centres set against a Ukrainian rural backdrop. As a result, it became increasingly rare to hear Ukrainian spoken in the towns like Hughesovka. Inevitably this ethnic melting pot led to friction and recurring clashes. The relations between Russians and Ukrainians were particularly strained in both towns and workers' settlements, leading to confrontations and frequent knife fights. The Tatars and Muslims were often the victims of violence by Slavs and almost every strike or labour protest in the Donbas ended in violent riots and large-scale anti-Jewish pogroms.[10] The situation in the Donbass at this time has been compared with the contemporary expansion westwards in the USA and Canada and the region was known as Russian America in the latter part of 19th century. Certainly there were similarities with a rapidly growing immigrant population drawn from a variety of nations and cultures, new opportunities and a feeling of lawlessness plus a dislike of distant central government. But the Donbass never really developed the same spirit of freedom or cultural values that characterised this period in northern America.

The Tsarist government's policies towards Ukraine with an emphasis on the development of its rich resources led to an unbalanced industrial structure. The railroad system expansion and transportation pricing encouraged the shipment of Ukraine's rich mineral, industrial, and agricultural raw materials resources to manufacturing centres elsewhere in Russia, primarily those in Moscow and St Petersburg. At the same time, the government's customs tariff policy also favoured the export of these same raw materials abroad. This discouraged the production of manufactured goods and general consumer products in Ukraine. By 1914, although Ukraine now accounted for around 20% of Russia's industrial output, it was almost exclusively heavy industry, largely financed by foreign investment.

---

10   Theodore Friedgut – ibid

Foreign-owned companies (mainly French, British, and Belgian) produced 70% of Ukraine's coal, 67% of its pig iron, 58% of its steel, and 100% of its machinery. The sugar industry was a notable exception being almost exclusively owned by local producers, many of them Ukrainian. At the start of the 20th century most of this industrial activity was centred in the Donbass with 12 large metallurgical plants plus more than 300 coal mines and smaller iron works. In the 30 years since Hughes' arrival, the region had been transformed from empty fields into the main coal, iron and steel centre of the Russian Empire.

Hughes was not the first British entrepreneur to commercially exploit the coal and iron resources of Ukraine. That distinction belongs to Charles Gascoigne (see page 175) who pre-dated Hughes by some 60 years. The Russian government had been aware for some time that there was coal in the Ukraine and the region's resources were one of the reasons behind the Tsarist Empire's expansion into the area. With control of the Ukraine established, the government turned its attention to expanding its coal and iron production by using Ukrainian coal. In 1794 an expedition led by Gascoigne was sent to the Donbass region to explore the region's possibilities and to choose a site for building an ironworks and coal mines. Gascoigne was impressed by the potential and selected a location near the river Lugan. In November 1795, Katherine II approved a bill for the establishment of coal mining and an iron smelting plant in the location selected by Gascoigne. Lugansk was to become the centre of a new metallurgical complex in this part of Russia using iron ore brought from the Urals. Construction of the new plant was started immediately under the direction of Gascoigne with a group of ten skilled British workers and some 200 locally recruited men. It took more than two years to complete the works and it produced its first iron (cannon shells) in 1798. Most of the British workers stayed on in a supervisory role and to train the Russians. Coal mining was also started nearby in 1796. But as Hughes found out later, hiring local workers was not easy and peasants were brought to Lugansk from many other parts of Russia and the jails were even used as a source of labour!

As the population of Lugansk grew, other manufacturing operations became established in the town in the same way that was to subsequently occur in Hughesovka. There were three brick making factories, one tile plant and five lard and candle making factories, plus a hospital, a school, works police, a prison and a play house. There were 204 brick houses, 20 wooden huts and 74 barracks for craftsmen and workers. The British specialists lived in their own colony on the main street known at the time as English street. So in many ways Lugansk was a much smaller version of what Hughes was to later achieve in Hughesovka. In the first half of the 19th century, the plant produced guns, shells, grenades and other kinds of armament, mostly for the Russian Black Sea fleet. The plant was an important part of the country's armaments industry producing munitions for the many wars of the 19th century in which the Russian Empire took part. It is ironic that much of the munitions used by the Russians fighting the British during the Crimean war were sourced from this British built and run plant. However the cost of production in Lugansk using iron from the Urals proved expensive and uncompetitive, limiting its further development.

At the start of the 19th century, Russia produced one third of the world's iron and was the largest exporter, much of it going to Britain. But as the century progressed, Russia lost much of its overseas iron markets and its overall economy developed more slowly than did that of the major European nations to its west. Although Russia's population was substantially larger than those of the more developed Western countries, the vast majority of the people lived in rural communities and engaged in relatively primitive agriculture. Industry, in general, had greater state involvement and control than in Western Europe but in certain sectors it was steadily developing with private initiative, some of it foreign. Between 1850 and 1900, Russia's population doubled, but it remained chiefly rural well into the 20th century. Russia's population growth rate from 1850 to 1910 was the fastest of all the major powers except for the United States.

It was clear to the Tsarist government in the 1860s that if current trends continued, Russia would become a second-class power and the security of the state would be threatened. But there were major obstacles to accelerating industrial development in the way seen earlier in Britain or Germany –

- Although the overall levels of literacy in Russia compared well with most of Europe, the country lacked a sizeable, educated and entrepreneurial middle class.
- Despite a fast-growing population, labour mobility was low and even after the emancipation of the serfs in 1861 it showed little sign of changing.
- The overall size of Russia meant that massive resources would be required to industrialise and these were not available in a poor, unsophisticated economy.
- Russia's external trade was relatively small, with most markets already served by other industrialised nations, so this was not an easy route for expansion or raising revenue.
- There were deep concerns in the ruling circles about the potential impacts on Russian society of industrialisation, especially the creation of a landless proletariat and rising political unrest in the growing cities.
- The country's industrial output was heavily dependent on a single region – the Urals – which was geographically poorly placed to fully serve Russia's needs.

Since many of the ruling elite were large land-owners, they did not see such change to be in their interest. The potential loss of peasants from the land plus the rise of power and influence of a new class of businessmen and financiers meant that many of them fought the government's new policies very strongly. Given this situation, the pace of Russian industrialisation was slow and hesitant, not

63

really taking off until the 1880s with the arrival of more foreign companies following Hughes' lead. Less than half of all coal and iron consumed in Russia in the 1870s was produced domestically and Britain was the main supplier of both. There were, however, some very successful industrialists in Russia by 1860 and there were probably more millionaires in St Petersburg and Moscow at this time than in New York.[11] But their attitudes towards economic development and industrial growth were mixed. Having made their fortune, many were only interested in reducing competition or becoming landed gentry and joining the nobility.

The following index of economic growth[12] shows the relative changes in population compared with agricultural and industrial growth between 1861 and 1913 –

	Industrial Production	Agricultural Production	Total Population
1861	100	100	100
1871	149	111	116
1881	252	112	136
1891	399	117	162
1901	750	181	183
1913	1165	309	232

Although the results in the table above appear to show substantial achievement, the country started from a low base and Russia could hardly be described as an industrialised economy by 1900, or even by the time of the revolution in 1917. In 1861, Russia's overall industrial output was comparable with other major European powers. By 1913 it was well ahead of France or Italy and close in size to that of Britain and Germany. But in terms of GDP – production per head of population, it was woefully behind and Russia failed to match the performance of most other European countries. The

---

11   William Blackwell – The Beginnings of Russian Industrialisation, 1968

12   J Bromley – Russia 1848-1917, 1970

primary reason for this was the failure of the country to utilise its substantial resources to develop its economy in line with its population growth, largely because the Tsarist government during this period failed to find successful solutions to the five problems outlined above. The total population of the Russian Empire grew from over 70 million in 1860 to 164 million by 1913. This rate of growth was only exceeded among the major economies of the world by the United States, where immigration was a major factor.

Between 1860 and 1890, annual coal production grew around 1,200% to over 6.6 million tonnes, and iron and steel production increased more than four times to two million tonnes per year. As a result, by the 1890s Russia's dependency on imported industrial products was greatly reduced. Only 1% of the rails and 20% of the rolling stock needed for the expansion of the railway system were sourced abroad. Ukrainian factories, notably John Hughes' New Russia Company, were now the primary suppliers. However, the impetus for this growth, especially in the mining and metallurgical sectors came from foreign companies and they continued to sustain Russia's industrial development up to the 1917 revolution. Their dominance can be seen in the following table showing the approximate proportion of foreign capital as a percentage of total Russian capital in 1914[13] –

Sector	Foreign Capital
Mining	90%
Metallurgy	40%
Textiles	28%
Commercial Banks	43%
Average	33%

There has been much discussion about the effectiveness of the state in accelerating the pace of Russian industrialisation in the second

13   J Bromley – ibid

half of the 19th century and the impact of the large amount of foreign investment. As has already been described, Russia recognised it had fallen behind most other European powers and needed to accelerate its pace of industrialisation. Despite some progress, primarily in textiles, entrepreneurship and business generally were held in low esteem in Tsarist Russia. Among those entrepreneurs that did exist, there also seemed to be a reluctance to set up new industries – a fact noted by several contemporary sources. In the 1860s the government understood that the country lacked skilled Russian entrepreneurs with the incentive and capital to rapidly develop the economy. It reasoned that if the government could provide the opportunity to exploit Russia's untapped resources for good profits, enhanced by a steady level of state demand and general encouragement from the sidelines, the international capitalist market system would respond. This approach was increasingly adopted and implemented in the latter part of the 19th century, especially under the finance minister Witte, with reasonable success. And the European capitalist market responded with a host of new companies set up by foreigners across Russia, bringing new capital, techniques and processes and most importantly, providing the security of domestic sourcing. Hughes and the New Russia Company were an early example of what could be achieved with this new policy. Clearly, state influence was important in the setting up of the New Russia Company and its expenditure on railways was of vital importance to the ongoing survival of the business. But even at the height of the railway boom between 1880 and 1900, the state spent less than 5% of its budget on railroad construction and even less on direct subsidies to emerging industries. Also, the government failed to do enough in other areas of the economy, in particular the use of truly competitive tenders for state contracts and reining in corruption by officials.

However, even this limited level of state expenditure was vital to most of those firms that were the favoured recipients of government contracts such as the New Russia Company. The beneficiaries generally prospered while others less fortunate struggled to stay in business due to the low levels of non-government demand in the economy. But it was not so easy for those few companies fortunate to receive state orders as the contracts were at a fixed price that would vary each year on a 'take it or leave' it basis. In the early 1900s for example, the state paid between 1.10 and 1.35 roubles per pud for steel rails – a significant price variation for companies to deal with and lower than the original price agreed with Hughes in 1870. It seems that the average price obtained on state rail orders provided at best a 20% return on sales[14] – hardly a fantastic return given the problems and risks of operating in Russia. The hoped for profits on the large initial capital investments made by foreign companies did not therefore always materialise. It largely depended on the decisions made by key government officials. As a result of this system, many of the new foreign ventures ran into financial problems and were purchased by Russians at low prices or forced to re-structure; some did not survive into the 20th century. For many companies it was not the quality or price of its products that mattered most but the quality of its government connections. In this respect, Hughes had benefited by assiduously nurturing his official contacts right from the start.

Despite these problems, foreign investment remained strong until 1914 by which date foreigners held over 30% of the capital of companies operating in Russia overall. The leading investors in Russia were the Germans, followed by the British. In the Ukraine region, the Belgians and French were more dominant. By the end of the 19th century, the British had become much more interested in the oil resources in the Caucasus region where they rapidly established themselves as by far the dominant investors. Overall, it seems fair to say that the impact of foreign entrepreneurs on Russia was favourable. As in the case of Hughes' New Russia Company, they brought much needed capital and investment in state-of-the-art equipment

---

14   John McKay – Pioneers for Profit, 1970

for new companies to exploit hitherto untapped resources. In doing so, they were also the catalyst for growth in the broader economy. They provided a secure domestic supply of vital goods, mostly at competitive world prices and trained Russian workers in new skills. Lastly, the vast majority of the profits generated by this economic activity stayed within Russia with expatriated dividends remaining generally low.

For a variety of reasons, by the 1860s the government found itself in control of a large part of the country's iron industry along with an already sizeable number of other state-run businesses, mostly in the armaments sector. Due to a lack of skilled managers and widespread corruption, production was inefficient, output was sold at inflated prices and many operations failed to make a profit for the state. As a British engineer involved in running Russian iron works at the time said, *'The whole system of government ... manufacture is rotten throughout.'*[15] The need for the Russian state to concentrate on government and not commerce was increasingly recognised and step-by-step attempts were made to transfer these enterprises to private ownership in the 1870s and beyond. However, the reform process did not survive into the 1880s. Although many of the changes already initiated continued to move the economy forward, the government failed to complete the work it had started and in some ways went backward. The absolutist system of government by the Tsar and state stifled true reform and private initiative. For the Russian state, control was everything; it became involved in or directed virtually all socio-economic activity. Russia carried on industrialising but the state proved ineffective at *modernising* the country and its institutions. Industrialisation was transforming society and society wanted a greater say in how it was governed. This failure of policy led to increasing disillusionment and discontent right across the country and was a major contributor to the 1917 revolution.

---

15   Herbert Barry – Russia in 1870, 1871

Due in large part to Russia's extensive land mass and harsh climatic conditions, transportation has always been a major problem for its people and government. Since early times, waterways had provided the majority of transportation for trade and people. Although Russia's river systems were extensive, connecting north to south and east to west, they could only be used when the rivers were not frozen. In southern Russia, the rivers freeze from three to four months each year and in northern Russia, they are ice-bound for six to seven months every year. In addition, some rivers were poorly maintained and in the summer months silting and sandbanks prevented the passage of all but the smallest of barges. As well as being slow, these systems were thus only usable for around six months each year. Goods that didn't reach their destination in time would either spoil or have to be stockpiled until the next season. The complete voyage from Astrakhan and the Lower Volga to St Petersburg often took two years to complete.

The road system in the 1800s was even worse. Those few roads that had been built were poorly maintained, often with broken bridges blocking the route. Most roads were made with sand on top of dirt. These became too muddy to be used much in wet weather, frozen ruts and snow made them impassable in winter and the sand formed deep drifts in dry, windy weather. Although several thousand miles of macadamised and wooden plank roads had been built, this was still a totally inadequate network for a country the size of Russia. The wooden plank road was a Russian innovation that was also taken up in parts of the USA and Canada in the 1830s. These slow and relatively inefficient transport methods, coupled with the great distances resulted in Russian traders having to provide extended credit terms to cover the long periods required to bring goods to market. This tied up scarce capital and increased overall costs.

Despite their proven efficiency for transportation over either waterways or roads, railroads had a slow start. Prior to the mid-1800s, very little consideration had been given to railroad construction in

Russia. A few mines and factories in the Urals used tramways to move ore or products but they used horses or men to pull the carts over short distances. Several plans were made to build railways, but none were accepted until the Austrian engineer von Gerstner pushed through his proposal in 1836 to build a railway line from St Petersburg to Tsarskoe Selo, the Tsar's summer resort. This first line using imported British rails was completed after 18 months and led a few years later to the more ambitious idea of a railway linking St Petersburg and Moscow. Completed after eight years of work in 1852, this line was a significant achievement with over 400 miles of double track. However, this first major railway project ran into financial difficulties (due to construction problems and corruption) and was only finished with the help of a loan from Barings Bank in London of £5.5 million.

Construction of the St Petersburg to Moscow railway was partly supervised by Major George Washington Whistler (1800-1849), a prominent American railroad engineer. After graduating from West Point he travelled to England to learn more about railroad technology before returning to the USA and building several railways there. In 1842 he was invited by the Russians to work as an advisory engineer on the Moscow to St Petersburg line with a handsome annual salary of 60,000 roubles. While working on this project, he contracted cholera and died in St Petersburg two years before the line was completed. He is credited with selecting the five-foot rail gauge still used in Russia and neighbouring countries. Whistler's eldest son was the famous painter James McNeill Whistler. See later comments about the Whistler family on page 101.

With the more proactive approach to industrial development of Alexander II's government, it was clear railways would have to significantly move up the agenda. Russia's then finance minister

Reutern wrote to Alexander II that *'without railways, Russia cannot be considered secure in her boundaries'*. Although the Tsarist government's primary interest in railways was the potential military benefit, it also believed that the introduction of technological innovations from abroad such as the railways would strengthen the existing social order, not weaken it. But there was considerable debate within Russia about the potential impact of industrialisation on the country – many were against it. Thus the Tsar and his government were much more cautious about the social and economic effects of railways than other countries. In addition, the government was only just recovering from the Crimean War debts and was reluctant to take on the burden of financing the cost of expanding the rail system. The interest on Russia's national debt amounted to £30 million in 1869/70 and the government was struggling to balance its annual budget, leaving it little room to finance growth and industrialisation. So it initially encouraged private investment (as with the Tsarskoe Selo line) and many railways were in fact constructed and run by private companies. They managed to raise money in the St Petersburg stock market and through other private investors. Indeed, as the network developed, speculative interest in the railways among some quarters of the public grew and in the late 1860s there was briefly something of a railway investment mania. A company called Dvigatel seeking capital of 500,000 roubles to construct railways for goods transport received 64 million in paid-up applications. Another company extending the Ivanovo line offered 12,000 shares and received applications for three and a half million. Some foreign companies also entered the market and obtained concessions from the government.

But these were exceptions and the original policy largely failed due to the scarcity of Russian capital plus the large amounts of investment required to construct railways over the great distances between major towns. Constructing a rail network was made even more difficult due to the existence of four different gauges in 1860 – a legacy of various foreign engineers who had helped build the lines (Austrian, Americans, French and finally German).

The state was forced into direct participation, providing direct investments of 53 million roubles plus guarantees and taking out loans of 1.8 billion roubles between 1861 and 1876. These loans were Russian government bonds placed through a consortium of European bankers, led by Barings in London. The government also introduced subsidies for rail and rolling stock production, as well as preferential import duties and the weight of state intervention remained vital and dominant. However, the overall amount committed by the government to railways from its annual budgets was still relatively small, averaging 5%.[16]

The Barings were very active in financing the Russian state in the 19th century and *'after 1815, most of the money obtained abroad by the Russian government came from the coffers of the houses of Baring and Rothschild in London'.*[17] Between 1818 and 1850 Barings alone raised some £15 million for the Russian government in bonds and loans and remained in contact even during the Crimean war.

Hughes knew from the very start of his enterprise in Russia that as long as the government continued spending on developing the rail network, his business would largely succeed or fail on the basis of securing a high percentage of the government rail contracts. With his coal and iron sources secure and a modern low cost works plus 'friends in high places', he had good cause for optimism in this respect. As it turned out, the New Russia Company achieved an average of around 30% of its sales from the government in the 19th century, mostly rails. This actually increased to over 80% in the recession of the early 1900s which was a primary factor in the survival of the company at this time. The company managed to

---

16   William Blackwell – ibid
17   Herbert Barry – ibid

consistently achieve one of the highest percentages of government business of any of his main competitors.

During the early years of the railway boom, in spite of high tariffs and contracts specifying the use of local iron, Russian companies were unable or unwilling to meet demand. Around 70% of the iron rails used were imported (mostly from Britain, along with coal). Britain, once an importer of Russian pig iron, was now the major supplier. In order to improve supply, the Tsarist government moved to allow duty free import of iron from 1868. In some ways this was not a favourable situation for Hughes to start his new company. With no duty protection, he would have to compete with the well established and more efficient overseas iron producers. But he did have the right to import the materials needed to construct his works duty free as well as a ten-year production subsidy from the government. The duty free decision was reversed for pig iron products by 1887, which boosted foreign investment in the Donetsk region. But by then rail production had moved on to steel and the New Russia Company was well established, fully able to withstand increased domestic competition.

The Russian government maintained a clear interventionist rail policy during this period, directing contracts to use domestic rails, controlling prices and tariffs to develop Russian production and vitally providing large orders to selected producers to support the costly change over from iron to steel rails. Hughes was successful in obtaining around 25% of state orders for steel rails during the late 1870s and the profits provided the cash to fund the new investments needed. The government's interventionist approach was hotly debated but it eventually brought results. In 1860 Russia had less than 1000 miles of railroad; by 1870 this had risen to almost 6,000 miles and in 1890 Russia's rail network had about 20,000 miles of track. Between 1890 and 1900 railroad mileage almost doubled, giving Russia the most track of any nation other than the United States. By the latter part of the 19th century, the New

Russia Company was accounting for around 15% of domestic steel rail production. The impacts on Russia's economy were enormous. Russia's coal, iron, steel, and oil production tripled between 1890 and 1900. Between 1860 and 1890, annual coal production grew about 1,200% to over 6.6 million tonnes and iron and steel production more than doubled to two million tonnes per year. The expansion of the Russian rail network, however, was never sufficient to meet potential demand for transport. Both coal and iron producers regularly claimed that they were unable to fully supply domestic requirements due to the inadequacies of the network and rolling stock. Their position was further hampered by the lack of priority (and therefore reliability) given to coal transport outside the winter period. The transport of grain and sugar beet to the large population centres was deemed to be more important at harvest time and these were precisely the primary markets for coal. In addition, the ongoing construction of the railways meant the transport of its own construction materials absorbed a significant percentage of capacity. Because of these problems, the New Russia Company's ease of access to its own iron and coal, without relying on the Russian rail network was a major advantage over many of its competitors. The railway boom continued until the worldwide slump in the first few years of the 20th century, though investment picked up again after 1909 when Russian industry boomed largely due to re-armament after the war with Japan.

The Russian word for a railway station, 'vokzal', is derived from the English word 'Vauxhall'. Early Russian rail engineers who visited England to study the development of its rail network were taken initially to Vauxhall station. From this, they erroneously assumed the generic English word for a station was Vauxhall and adopted the same term on their return to Russia.

Prior to the emancipation of serfs in 1861, not all Russian peasants were serfs but all peasants were bound to the land on which they lived, obliged to pay their taxes and to provide military recruits to the state. After 1861, the government's intention was to gradually transform the freed serfs into peasants, each owning an individual plot of land in their village. These arrangements proved very unsatisfactory to the peasants for several reasons. Firstly, their share of the village land was often insufficient to keep them above the level of grinding poverty. Only around one third of the total area of agricultural land was allocated to the village communities, with the rest being retained by the state, Imperial family and the nobility. Also, the landowners often kept the best land for themselves, giving up only the poorest parts of their estates to the peasants. Secondly, the cost of buying their plots of land proved to be higher than the annual dues formerly paid to the landowners. Thirdly, the village communities kept the village land as collective property so as the population increased, the share of land available to each peasant became smaller and smaller. The rapid population growth in the latter half of the 19th century placed growing pressure on the available land and the standard of living, especially in western Russia and Ukraine. Thus after the emancipation, peasant discontent actually increased instead of falling and peasant riots continued through into the 20th century. This discontent, plus mounting debts from land purchases, caused an increasing number of peasants to leave their traditional rural communities and head for Siberia or Russia's expanding cities. This enormous movement of people was greatly facilitated as the empire's rail network grew. Russia's population grew from 74 million in 1858 to 128 million in 1897 and 178 million in 1914. Eighty percent of the population were peasants and 40% of these were former serfs or their descendants. Abraham Lincoln once said, *'God loves the common people, therefore he has made so many of them.'* God would have felt at home in Russia in the latter half of the19th century.

Although the lot of the peasants did slowly improve after the 1861 emancipation, the conditions encountered by Hughes on his arrival in Russia were generally closer to those of Britain 50 to 60 years before. Housing was primitive, at least outside the main towns. The main elements of the peasant diet were black bread and cabbage soup supplemented by whatever home-grown vegetables or fruit were in season. Meat was a rare luxury. Quass, a type of beer fermented from a mixture of bread and water, was the main drink. Healthcare was minimal and infant mortality was high – in rural areas more than half the children died within 12 months of birth. Conversely, in a Darwinian-like process, those that survived the early rigours of Russian life tended to be healthy and robust. Farming was mostly un-mechanised and peasants generally worked their plots on a subsistence basis, with any surplus going to local markets. Movement away from the immediate locality, whether temporary or permanent, was controlled by the village communes and complete freedom of movement was not granted until 1906.

Few peasants in rural areas could read or write. This was not due to an absence of any interest in education but rather the lack of opportunity. The Russian school system was run by the Orthodox church and families were expected to pay for the education of their offspring. The few schools that existed in the villages were usually run by local priests in a very haphazard manner – more often closed than open. The same fate often applied to the universities which were frequently shut by the state due to concerns about seditious behaviour. State education for children of both the Jewish and Polish minorities was specifically limited by government decree to 5% and 10% respectively. Thus the construction of 'factory' schools by Hughes and other industrialists was both a real benefit as well as a necessary step in providing education for the influx of peasants to their towns.

All the towns and villages had much the same appearance across Russia. Contemporary writers describe the villages as being mostly drab and cheerless, with unpaved and largely unlit streets. One British visitor in 1882 wrote –

'The wooden cottages of the peasantry have a dirty tumble-down appearance; the roads are mere tracks; the clearings, scratched with a primitive plough, produce, probably, the minimum crop of which the soil is capable; the snake-fences serve rather to indicate boundaries than to keep in or out any living thing, while the bearded Russian moujik (peasant), *in his greasy sheepskin and high boots, looks a ragged object beside the peasant or farmer across the border'* (in Germany)[18].

The small single-storey houses were usually not much more than wooden huts without gardens or flowers. Inside the sepia dullness of the interior, the long winter months would be spent close to the stove in the main room. This served as kitchen, living space and sleeping quarters with berths for the whole family arranged on or around the stove. In the hot summer months, this room was largely abandoned as most activities took place outdoors. Water was usually obtained from wells and sanitation systems were virtually non-existent. In the towns, houses were more substantial but still mostly made of wood, although often decorated with carved friezes and shutters. The homes of the richer merchants, local dignitaries and government buildings were built from stuccoed brick. There would be one or two hotels (usually of poor quality) and several solid whitewashed churches with a bell tower. Most large towns had a good market, a theatre plus a merchants' club, where gambling was very popular. But for the majority of peasants these facilities were inaccessible, apart from perhaps an occasional visit to the market.

---

18   John Baddeley – Russia on the Eighties, 1921

CHAPTER FIVE
Bigger and Better

Over the course of the next two years, the various technical problems that so nearly killed the project at birth were resolved and in September 1872 initial production tests began and the first iron rails were successfully rolled 12 months later. Production moved forwards and in 1874, the furnace was in almost constant action, producing pig iron at a rate of 7,500 tonnes per year (over 50% higher than the company's formal obligation to the government) plus 8,000 tonnes of iron rails. Although some technical issues continued to be experienced and labour shortages hampered progress, a second furnace was completed that year to further boost capacity. The new furnace was constructed using bricks made from fire-resistant clay found on site – yet a further benefit of Hughes' choice of location. By now, Hughes had augmented the number of British workers by employing several skilled Germans, Italians and Finns who had been working elsewhere in Russia. But although these men had either engineering or industrial experience, they were unfamiliar with the modern techniques Hughes was attempting to introduce and he concluded that he would have to train everyone regardless of previous experience. An analysis of the company's workforce at the end of 1874 provides an interesting insight into the mix of trades and activities underway at this stage of the company's development. Some 550 men were employed in the iron works and 370 in the mines but the largest group of 700 were in construction, haulage and other support operations and a further 180 were in agriculture. The latter accounted for 10% of the total workforce and were employed at the company farm producing food for the growing settlement.

Around this time, Hughes acquired a government contract from a failed Russian company to refurbish steel rails plus the rights to establish a new rail-producing factory. This astute move neatly eliminated a potential competitor while at the same time giving his company early exposure to steel rail technology. The company was now working seven local coal seams and had 12 coke ovens in operation. The small original settlement grew steadily to 800 workers at the end of 1872, 1295 in 1874 and around 2,000 workers by 1876. In that year, production of iron had risen to over 16,000 tonnes and the New Russia Company's works was now the largest of its kind in Russia.

With production in full swing, not everything went smoothly and the company did experience some quality problems. One third of the first batch of rails produced in 1873 were rejected, though this fell to 10% in 1874 and 5% by 1876 as Hughes and his team improved manufacturing processes and worker training. The delays and quality problems, however, did provide fuel for the many hostile officials who for various reasons did not want to see this foreign experiment succeed. Hughes was criticised in several government reports as not doing enough and being incapable of meeting his commitments. Such negative findings must have increased the mental pressure on Hughes, making his life more difficult than it already was. Rumours also started to circulate locally that all the cast iron produced by the New Russia Company had in fact been imported from England and passed off as their own product. The rumours were put about by government mining engineers jealous of the growing success of Hughes. They were picked up by the press and a cartoon even appeared in a Russian paper showing Hughes standing on top of a hill on the way back to England, carrying a large bag of subsidized gold over his shoulder. These rumours finally reached Grand Duke Constantin in St Petersburg, who had originally encouraged Hughes to set up his company. On a visit to the Black Sea, he decided to carry out an inspection of the company's operations. George Hume describes what then happened in his book[19] –

'On this visit being announced, Mr. Hughes requested me to come over to the works so as to assist him at the interview, he having sent Mr. Cameron to Taganrog in order to meet and accompany the Grand Duke to Hughesovka. At the date named the Grand Duke came to the station of Constantinovka, accompanied by Admiral Popoff ... and the leading mining engineers, many of whom had been the authors of the criticisms. On his arrival it was evident that the Duke was in a very excited condition. When alighting he took not the slightest notice of Mr. Hughes, with whom he was well acquainted, and after pacing up and down the platform for a short time re-entered his carriage, which was shunted on to a side line for the night. Admiral Popoff having made arrangements for the visit to take place next day, we entered the special train that the Company had provided and returned to Hughesovka.

The next morning the Grand Ducal party arrived and were accom-modated upon a trolley (on which chairs had been placed with the usual accompaniment of red baize) in order to go to the centre of the works, where carriages and a tent awaited them. Mr. Hughes had arranged that an inspection of the mine should first take place, after which they passed through every stage from the coke-ovens to the blast-furnace. This had been made ready for immediate casting on their arrival. The furnace being tapped, the molten metal poured forth into the moulds, when the Grand Duke, after asking to see the ores from which it was produced, called the chief of the Mining Department to him, and in severe tones asked him whether the material pouring from the furnace had been derived from the ores which had been shown him.

19   George Hume – ibid

80

Seldom in my experience have I seen a man so thoroughly humiliated, while undergoing the stern and well-merited censure of the Grand Duke, after he had been forced to admit that all his previous statements had no foundation in fact.

After his departure, a Kharkov paper announced that he had been so disappointed with the condition of the works that he had refused the lunch provided for him. As a matter of fact he had lingered so long, and had been so interested over the inspection, that the railway time-table did not permit of his staying any longer. The express train had been stopped at Constantinovka specially for him. From that time forward the relations with the governing authorities became satisfactory, and the Government inspectors were withdrawn.'

It seems the Duke's visit and positive reactions silenced the majority of Hughes' critics for the time being. As the company grew, so did its supporting infrastructure. The company had to be largely self-sufficient, capable of building and repairing most of its own machinery. To this end, workshops were built and more skilled men recruited from Britain. Another priority was to expand the brickworks to provide materials to build more homes for the growing settlement as well as lining the new furnaces. The company's trading arrangements also expanded. Iron ore was still mined locally but it was now being considerably supplemented by the use of scrap iron, mostly reject rails brought to Hughesovka from other parts of Russia and re-cast. Hughes was able to use the Ukraine river system to some extent for this as well as bringing some goods inland from the Azov Sea direct to Hughesovka.

Coal production had also increased to meet the rising demand from the works and was delivered on factory-owned railway lines using steam-powered locomotives. But Hughes was well aware from his time in Merthyr and Newport that steam engines had a greater use than just rail transport and he is credited with making various improvements to their design and operation. By the end of 1876, he had installed 22 steam-powered engines in the works and the company's 12 coke ovens were linked to the furnace by an overhead cable system. As with virtually all major equipment, these engines were imported from Britain, mainly hauled overland from the coast and assembled on site. They were a costly but important factor in raising production and reducing costs. As in so many areas, Hughes led the way in the efficient use of steam (and later electric) power in his operations. The New Russia Company was to consistently average the highest total horsepower and horsepower per worker of all companies in the Donbass. By now, Hughes was writing to the Russian government claiming that he had excess capacity and the company ran the risk of losing money. He was more confident now about the quality of his local workforce and believed that with more state orders, he could easily raise production, especially pig iron, thereby increasing employment to over 3,000 workers.

The strategic importance to the Russians of Hughes' rapidly expanding works became even more evident when war broke out between Russia and Turkish Ottoman Empire in 1877. In the period between the accession of Peter the Great in 1689 and the end of Romanov rule in 1917, Russia fought eight wars (1695-1696, 1711, 1735-1739, 1768-1774, 1787 -1792, 1806-1812, 1828-1829, and 1877-1878) either singly or with allies against the Ottomans. The 1877 war's origins lay in a rise in nationalism in the Balkans as well as Russia's desire to recover territorial losses it had suffered during the Crimean war and re-establish itself in the Black Sea. By supporting the political movements attempting to free Balkan nations from the Ottoman Empire, Russia saw its chance to extend its sphere of influence. The main theatre of battle was around the Danube and into Romania, with more limited action in Georgia and Armenia. Although the Turks generally had better weaponry, the Russians and their allies benefited from superior numbers and gradually gained the upper hand. Under pressure from the British the Russians and Turks agreed a peace treaty early in 1878 under which the Ottoman Empire recognized the independence of

Romania, Serbia, Montenegro, and the autonomy of Bulgaria and the Russians extended influence around the Black Sea.

The war emphasised Russia's need to reduce its dependence on imported strategic goods such as the large quantities of coal and iron from Britain through the Black Sea. It also once again demonstrated the need to improve its armaments industry plus the railway network and these objectives would be best achieved with greater domestic production of coal and iron. The growing output from the New Russia Company now looked even more attractive to the government, which partly explains its continued support for Hughes with a high number of contracts.

The 1877 Russian-Turkish war originated the division in the emblems of the International Red Cross and Red Crescent movements. Both Russia and the Ottoman Empire had signed the First Geneva Convention in 1864 which made the Red Cross, a colour reversal of the flag of neutral Switzerland, the sole emblem of protection for military medical personnel and facilities. However, the red cross reminded the Ottomans of the Crusades; so they elected to adopt the Red Crescent instead which ultimately became the accepted symbol for most Muslim countries.

As Hughes ramped up his production, he found not only was competition at home and from overseas growing but the market was changing too; iron was fast becoming obsolete as the industry worldwide changed over to the safer, more durable steel rails. The first steel rails had been laid at Crewe railway station in England as early as 1861. As already noted, this change in world markets had a severe impact on South Wales and Merthyr Tydfil especially. In 1877, three of the existing four iron works in Merthyr closed causing great hardship in the town. With little alternative employment, this meant real poverty and even famine for many local families and various appeals were made for assistance across the UK and overseas. The British workers in Hughesovka responded and in 1877 they raised a total of 378 roubles (approximately £50) which was sent in three separate instalments to Merthyr. A list of the contributors to the first instalment of almost £24 made in February 1878 shows some 70 names, headed by John Hughes. The levels of individual contributions were significant, given the average wages of these men, and they clearly show the depth of sympathy and support for friends and families back in Wales.

To speed up the move from iron to steel, the Russian government took action on three fronts. First in 1874 it took the decision to subsidise the Putilov factory in St Petersburg to re-equip itself to produce steel rails using the Bessemer process. Then in 1876, it introduced protective tariffs on imported steel rails providing a benefit for domestic producers of around one third of their selling price. Lastly, to further encourage the market, it started awarding generous contracts to those Russian works that could supply steel rails, including the now re-equipped Putilov works. With these policies in place, domestic production rose quickly accounting for 70% of demand for steel rails in Russia by the end of the decade.

With the significant benefit of the government subsidy to change to steel and subsequent large orders for steel rails, the Putilov works became a major early competitor for Hughes and its steel output surpassed that of the New Russia Company. By the 20th century it had moved more into producing rolling stock for the railways plus armaments and in 1916 started turning out armoured cars using imported Austin chassis from Britain. In 1917 it was at the centre of the Bolshevik revolution and Lenin spoke there in support of its striking workers.

These were dramatic changes in the rules. If the New Russia Company was to survive and continue to prosper, Hughes had to modernise and move over from iron to steel. This was a major challenge for the company, both technically and financially. Although the business was now profitable and making good returns, the costs involved in such a changeover would be very significant. Also, adapting the production processes after only a few years of iron making would put a big strain on both the workforce and management. Hughes, with his small band of British workers, had been at the forefront of successful commercial coal mining and modern iron production methods and the New Russia Company was the first to use coking coal for smelting iron in southern Russia. They had effectively been responsible for introducing the Industrial Revolution to this part of the world. Now, after just a few short years, they found themselves behind in the technological race.

The changeover to steel was to take the company three years to successfully master, even though Hughes had time to prepare for it. As with the production of iron rails earlier, there were technical and quality problems as well as difficulties using the local iron ore. Monthly output both in the mines and at the works fluctuated considerably and for several months at the end of 1878, no rails were produced at all, causing havoc with cash flow and production planning. Once again the Russian sceptics were quick to criticise, doubting Hughes' ability to produce steel in the quantities required from the local ores. But by 1881, the output of steel rails was up to the previous levels of iron rails and, thereafter, with the exception of the 1884 downturn, steadily increased. This turbulent period for the company placed a great strain on the company's resources and may have been behind Hughes' later comments about closing the company in 1885 – see page 171. This conversion from iron to steel was both expensive and difficult for the company and no further major investment occurred until after Hughes' death in 1889. Financing this changeover was achieved by using the company's accumulated retained profits and the issue of new shares. By 1879 the number of shareholders had risen to 46 of which 16 were now Russian nationals, including Count Etienne Hendrikoff and Alexander Boritorovski, a government privy councillor in St Petersburg.

The need to change from iron production to steel presented Hughes with an important choice of technology. The original process, invented by Bessemer in 1856, would have been more familiar to Hughes as it had been used extensively in South Wales to manufacture steel rails and so would have been easier and quicker to adopt. The more recent method was the Siemens-Martin system introduced a decade later. This was an open-hearth process that took more time but was more fuel efficient and resulted in a higher quality steel. Hughes decided to go with the Siemens process initially and by 1884 the company had installed three open-hearth blast furnaces and annual steel production reached 20,000 tonnes. The reason for Hughes selecting the Siemens process over the cheaper Bessemer one was probably mainly driven by the need to maintain high quality. All rails supplied to the Russian government had to pass very exacting standards and testing was done on site by government engineers. Given the importance of the government contracts to the New Russia Company, Hughes could not afford to fall down on quality. As with many things, his decision proved to be the right one in the long run (even though the Bessemer system was added by Hughes' sons much later in 1898). The Siemens process soon became the standard for much of the industry worldwide. Its introduction by Hughes to the Ukraine proved to be enduring as even today 50% of its steel is produced by the open-hearth system – the highest share in the world.

As Hughesovka's production continued to increase in the 1880s, the local iron ore deposits were proving to be inadequate both in quantity and quality and a growing regional trade network was established of coal for iron and steel. Initially, this was with Krivoi Rog, some 230 miles to the west of Hughesovka. The existence of significant iron ore deposits in this area had been known for some years having been accidentally discovered by Alexander Pol', a Ukrainian in 1866 during archaeological research. However, it was not until the early 1880s that the area's potential began to be exploited thanks to foreign investment. In 1881 a French company began to work the local iron-ore deposits and after lengthy discussions a railway was eventually constructed to the Donets Basin coalfield in 1884, allowing easier access to this major source of iron. Hughes was quick to move to take advantage of this important resource and set up his own mines, purchasing the rights from local land owners.

The Krivoi Rog ore was of relatively high quality, yielding up to 65% pure iron. This was comparable with the Urals deposits and much richer than the iron ore used in much of Western Europe at that time which only averaged 30 to 40% purity. This gave an important cost benefit to The New Russia Company (and later, additional foreign iron makers who were soon to enter the region) as the output from their furnaces would be significantly higher per tonne of ore used. By the early 20th century, the new Russia Company was employing around 500 men at its iron mines in Krivoi Rog, managed by a Mr Perry from England who lived there with his wife and family. The company put great effort into introducing new mining techniques to increase production as well as continuously exploring for new deposits. This activity was mirrored in the coal mines in Hughesovka and was part of a strategic long-range approach to the business, ensuring its ongoing production capability by only relying on its own resources. The linking of Krivoi Rog iron to the Donets Basin coalfields was one of the most important steps in the development of southern Ukraine as the new centre of Russia's metallurgical industry. By 1910 the region's iron and steel production was more than three times that of the Urals, and the Ekaterinoslav district alone (including the New Russia Company) accounted for almost 50% of the empire's steel output.

By the mid 1890's however, there were concerns about the possible early depletion of the Krivoi Rog reserves as well as its escalating price. Between 1895 and 1898, the ore price doubled, following demands for increased royalties from the Russian owners and the need to mine deeper underground. This led to the eventual development of the much larger iron ore deposits in the Kerch peninsular on the Azov Sea. However, the quality of the ore was much lower than that in Krivoi Rog and it took several years of pioneering work by two Belgian companies to sort out the technical difficulties in using this new source. In its final years, the New Russia Company also explored the feasibility of obtaining supplies of high-grade iron ore from the recently discovered deposits at Magnitogorsk in the southern Urals.

The port of Kerch sits strategically on an isthmus connecting the south side of the Azov Sea and the Black Sea. During the Crimean War the city had been devastated by British forces but in the late 19th century, its prime commercial position coupled to its mineral resource led to considerable economic re-development and by 1900, Kerch was connected to the main Russian railroad system. The Donetsk-Krivoi Rog Soviet Republic was a short-lived Soviet republic with its capital initially in Kharkov. Established by Bolsheviks in February 1918, it was not recognized by anyone, including the Russian Soviet Republic. Lasting only a couple of months, it was then incorporated into the new Ukrainian SSR. The republic had its own flag of black, blue and red horizontal stripes and claimed the territories south of the neighbouring Ukrainian People's Republic, covering the Kharkov, Donbass and Ekaterinoslav governorates and therefore the town of Hughesovka.

One of the main differences between the New Russia Company and other similar foreign enterprises that were steadily springing up in southern Russia was that Hughes' business was not linked to an established parent company in the home country. Virtually all his main competitors were set up by large European steel makers which gave them the advantage of being able to draw more easily on technical expertise, skilled manpower, logistical support, capital and access to other markets. The fact that the New Russia Company survived and prospered against such strong international competition is a tribute to the skills and energy of Hughes and his British managers. Although few company records still exist, a copy of the 1883 balance sheet has survived which shows how well the company had performed during its first 12 years of operations.

The company's balance sheet for December 31st 1883 showed –

Fixed Assets (land, buildings, railways, houses etc.)	£721,553
Stock & work in progress	£180,949
Debtors	£353,976
Cash in hand	£192,507
Dividend	£22,500
Net Assets	**£1,471,485**

5571 Ordinary shares of £50	£278,550
429 Preference shares of £50	£21,450
Total	**£300,000**

Obligations (interest) @ 5%	£147,000
Mortgage obligations @ 6%	£163,000
Total	**£310,000**

Unappropriated shares	£200,000
Government loan (due in 1900)	£35,234
Creditors	£314,135
Deposits and advances	£175,321
Bills of exchange	£54,629
Total	**£779,319**
Carried forward	£82,168
Balance	**£1,471,485**

These accounts are interesting for several reasons. They clearly illustrate the company had grown into a very profitable operation – the original £300,000 share capital had grown into net assets of close to £1.5 million (close to £150 million today), almost a five-fold increase. This probably represented at the time the largest single investment in the Ukraine. Also of the 1,000 original preference shares issued to Hughes and John Gooch in 1870, less than half remain, the balance presumably having been repurchased by the company. The figures also show how the profits generated in the early years were retained to fund investment in new infrastructure and equipment needed for the expansion of the works and the town. The dividend payment of £22,500 shown above is believed to be the very first dividend declared by the company, confirming that the New Russia Company was being prudently run as a long-term investment, not to earn quick, speculative profits as some of the other foreign firms that arrived in the Donbass in the late 1880s.

Notes to these accounts show that of the £82,168 shown as being carried forward, almost £50,000 was earmarked for a further dividend, giving a proposed return of 15% to the preference shareholders and 25% to ordinary shareholders. It's also interesting to see the relatively large amount of cash held by the company. This may well have been due to the timing of wage payments – a major cash outlay for the company each month. Although there is a lack of clarity concerning the amount and timing of subsequent dividends actually paid by the company due to the absence of detailed records, most contemporary sources talk of very high dividend returns being achieved. A list for a ten-year period around the turn of the century gives the following dividends paid out each year by the New Russia Company[20] – 19%, 16%, 28%, 30%, 24%, 125%, 15%, 20%, 25% and 20%. In addition, the shareholders had further benefited from at least one share split during this period.

---

20   Sir Henry Norman – All The Russias, 1902

What is certain is the fact that the company's reputation for having earned high profits encouraged other foreign companies to come to south Russia to invest in its coal and iron resources. The Belgian company Cockerill, who became one of the largest and most successful investors in the Russian steel industry, carefully studied the New Russia Company's figures before taking the decision to set up a company in Ukraine in 1885. They concluded that profit levels of 20-30% on capital invested would be possible. Far from fearing these new foreign entrants to the Russian market, Hughes actually encouraged them to follow his lead. With his sources of iron and coal secure and confident in his government contacts for future business, Hughes believed that the new companies would strengthen the position of south Ukraine as the pre-eminent metallurgical centre in Russia, in turn improving its infrastructure and relationships with the Tsarist regime. Hughes was looking at the broader benefits for Russia, not the potentially adverse impacts on his own company. This was not the first time that Hughes had adopted such a position; he was genuinely concerned about improving the state of Russian industry and its international competitiveness. Hughes' company blazed the trail in Russia by demonstrating the commercial sense of full integration in modern steel making. Only by combining secure coal supplies with the smelting, refining and processing of quality ores in a high capacity steelworks and an integrated transport system could optimum efficiency and profits be attained. The New Russia Company had become the benchmark for others to emulate and eventually surpass. It was this structure that was to drive southern Russia into becoming one of the leading coal, iron and steel producing regions in the world by the end of the 19th century. The enterprises established by mostly foreign entrepreneurs pushed one of the most backward regions in the Russian Empire to being one of the most productive, along with a modernised society.

Developments in coal production in the Donbass largely went hand in hand with those in metallurgy and again Hughes led the way.

Until the 1890s, when other large foreign entrepreneurs entered the market, there were only two large foreign owned coal mines in Donets – that of Hughes and the nearby French Rutchenko mine, opened in 1873. A few smaller mines remained owned and operated by private individuals, including one owned by Thomas James from Wales. Until the 1890s, apart from the New Russia Company, the majority of coal mined in the region was used as fuel by the railways or the large Ukrainian sugar mills. Hughes showed the logic of self-sufficiency by using his own local coal and converting it into coke to power his own iron and steel works.

The Donets coal deposits were immense – hundreds of millions of tonnes – with multiple workable seams. Prior to the arrival of Hughes, the majority of coal mines were small, often working outcrops and only seasonally operated to allow the peasant workers to return to their farms. Many were owned by absentee landlords living in Moscow or Kharkov. Their mines were left in charge of relatively junior personnel and equipment was minimal with poor productivity. Although this meant production could be flexible and capital investment minimised resulting in low costs, it was wasteful and the quality was variable. Also, the cutting of coal remained largely a manual operation in most Russian mines with only 60 drills in use in 1912 compared with 16,000 in the USA. The issue of absentee landlords and a lack of entrepreneurial spirit was a significant barrier to industrial progress throughout Russia in the 19th century. Large landholdings containing rich deposits of both coal and iron were rarely developed into efficient profitable businesses. Their owners were simply content to live off the income from these estates and not take risks or get their hands dirty. The extensive Nizhny Tagil iron works near Perm in the Urals owned by the wealthy Demidov family had only been visited once by its owners in over 20 years [21].

---

21   Herbert Barry – Russian Metallurgical Works, 1870

As the New Russia Company expanded, its need for ever greater quantities of coal meant deeper seams had to be worked and productivity increased. Of the 60,000 acres of land owned by the company, about half was coal bearing. Hughes brought modern coal mining methods to the region and showed the benefits of capital investment and improved management in integrated, large-capacity mines. Ventilation systems were installed and power brought to the pithead for pumps and winding gear with drills being introduced at the coal face. Not everyone was convinced, however, of the benefits, especially Russian-owned mines. They felt the new methods were too sophisticated for their workers and the investments would not pay for themselves and so many remained small-scale producers. Contemporary estimates indicate that even as late as the 1880s, fully half of the miners were still seasonal workers. Despite huge reserves, the fragmented, inefficient domestic industry, hampered by a poor distribution system, was unable to meet increasing demand. Although coal production steadily rose, imports remained important in Russia throughout the 19th century, especially from Britain. The British dominated the import trade through the Azov Sea ports as well as across the whole Black Sea region, delivering coal at very competitive prices. The fact that English ships coming to load grain in the Ukrainian ports brought coal as ballast significantly helped their position. Hughes was well aware of this and as early as 1874 he wrote to the Russian government requesting improved regional rail links to Hughesovka claiming he could increase output to re-place much of the British imports. These did not really decline in southern Russia until the late 1880s when duties were imposed on imported coal. With the influx of other foreign firms during the 1890s, coal production soared 400% and the production of coke (for steel making) rose even faster. By 1900 there were around 4,000 coke ovens in south Russia but the market was dominated by the New Russia Company and four or five other foreign-owned firms.

As with coal mines the world over, safety was always an important issue. In Russia, the safety record was poor, largely due to the low levels of investment and fragmented nature of the industry. From the outset, Hughes recognised that by investing in better ventilation, increased mechanisation and pumps, he would achieve greater coal production as well as higher levels of safety in his mines. A mine safety and rescue group was formed and equipped and it saw action on several occasions. Indeed, the New Russia Company's contribution to improved mine safety was cited in an award it received in 1896. There was also a more practical reason for reducing fatal accidents – the complications of the police enquiries that followed a death. These could drag on for months, often leading to a trial and the foreign owner of any business involved in such an incident could not leave the country.

In theory the development of all Russian towns was governed by the Urban Statute of 1785 but by the time of Hughes' arrival, it was consistently being ignored. The settlement that initially grew up around the works was largely unplanned with the location of any buildings or streets largely determined in relation to their working function. But within a few years it started to become more organised with a sense of purpose and structure. By the mid 1870s, Hughesovka had acquired many of the basic amenities of any town – cafes, taverns, a 12-bed hospital, a chemist, a Sunday market where prices were no higher than in the main city of Kharkov and inevitably a small police force. There was also an 'English style' hotel (which is still in use today), equipped with snooker tables that were very popular with both the British and Russians. The Russians have their own version of billiards, which is played on the same size of table but they use larger and heavier balls with 15 white numbered balls and a red cue ball. As the town grew, it developed into roughly three parts, the factory and mines area to the south, then the commercial and 'English' sections which was known as Novyi Svet (New World) on the rising land overlooking the Kalmius river and to the north, and the Russian quarter with the indoor market, inns, churches and police station. The latter quarter was known to the locals by names such as Shanghai

Hughesovka's main streets in the 1890s *(GRO)*

A boot maker's shop in the 1980s - note the street lamp *(GRO)*

Hughesovka's main pharmacy

Company workers cottages with gardens *(GRO)*

Workers' housing in the British quarter *(GRO)*

Senior manager's company house *(GRO)*

Winter transport *(GRO)*

Hughesovka's Orthodox church *(GRO)*

A street market in Hughesovka *(GRO)*

Medical staff and patients outside the hospital *(GRO)*

Hospital facilities – early 20th century

and the Kennels, reflecting the type of housing and overcrowded, unhealthy nature of the district. Local traders, craftsmen and government officials also tended to live in this section. The centre of Hughesovka was laid out in blocks, similar in design to the grid system of North American towns. The streets were called 'lines', each one being numbered, with the broad principal streets running north to south. The main street, from the steelworks to the railway station, would eventually extend for more than five miles in length. Like most Russian towns at the time, the streets were initially unpaved; dusty in summer, frozen in the winter and very muddy in the spring. The more important streets were covered with waste slag from the works to provide a better surface although this tended to increase the dust levels in summer. However, by 1913 electric lighting had been installed along the main streets in Novyi Svet as well as around parts of the works and by then the town benefited from some 13 miles of pavement. Refuse incinerators were built along the main residential streets to reduce rubbish and improve sanitation and alleys between the blocks of houses made it easier to collect refuse and human waste. However, the need to avoid areas liable to subsidence from early coal mining led to a somewhat patchy expansion of the growing residential and factory areas.

The early town buildings were all of simple design and construction but with the need for larger and more sophisticated buildings by the 1880s, the company was employing its own resident architect called Moldingauer. He was responsible for the layout of many of the new housing areas as well as designing several of the more prominent homes in Hughesovka including the house of Archibald Balfour and that of the Hughes family, completed in the 1880s. The Hughes' family house was a large impressive building. Contemporary photos show a solid double-fronted, two-storied home built largely from brick with porticos at the entrance and a first-floor balcony with balustrade. It lay at the end of the main street in the southern part of town, between the works and the factory hospital and had a large walled garden looking out south-eastwards over the river to the open steppe beyond.

As resident manager of the New Russia Company, Hughes effectively controlled everything that happened in respect of the town's development. There was a 'bazaar office' that issued decrees controlling various aspects of daily life but this committee was appointed and financed by the company. All commercial and construction activity had to be approved by the company as were all leases and rents. However, there is no evidence to suggest that Hughes used this absolute power to the detriment of the town, apart from one issue discussed later. It never seems to have been a barrier to growth and in practice was probably at least as efficient as the town council system in 'normal' Russian provincial towns. In fact, Hughes seems to have encouraged development and home ownership, knowing the benefits these would bring to the town and the company. Towards the end of the 1880s, residential plots were offered on favourable leases to those wishing to build their own houses, whether company employees or not. When it later became necessary to redevelop one of these sites for factory expansion *Hughes offered to move the houses that had been built there to new sites in the Novyi Svet at his own expense, paying an indemnity of 20% of the houses' value in addition to this*.[22] However, the canny Hughes never lost control of the company's land – it was always leased, never sold. The company's accounts showed a dramatic rise in rental receipts from 40,000 roubles in 1891 to 600,000 roubles in 1905.

By 1900 the company had some 50 miles of its own rail track in use in the town and a second railway link was built connecting Hughesovka to Mushketovo, a few miles to the southeast. The ability to travel easily by rail became an important factor in the continuing economic and social development of the town and

---

22 Theodore Friedgut – ibid

Hughesovka's stations were some of the busiest in the Donbass, used by tens of thousands of passengers each year. As the town developed further, other commercial activities were gradually established including factories producing agricultural equipment and domestic and industrial clothing. The presence of the latter encouraged the Singer Sewing Machine Company to open a branch. Given the importance of Hughesovka in the region's mining and metallurgy industries, other companies active in these sectors set up operations there. A factory manufacturing mine cables was established by British investors, and several agencies for the marketing and distribution of national and international brands of tools and equipment were established.

Like much of the Donbass, the absence of rain for long periods during the summer months in Hughesovka became an increasing problem. In 1890 the company built a dam on the river Kalmius at a cost of 100,000 roubles, creating a lake to supply water for the works and the town. The lake provided an added bonus for recreation, skating in winter and boating in summer. Horse-drawn water bowsers were used to distribute water in the town and to spray the streets to keep the dust down. However, the water was very hard and caustic soda had to be used as a softener in the works – about one tonne per month, most of it imported from England until the 20th century. The general water shortage in the Donbass was an important contributor to the poor sanitation of all the towns in the region, leading to disease and periodic epidemics.

Although the early 1880s saw a downturn in the Russian economy, Hughes continued to expand, adding a third blast furnace in 1884, and the company was mining close to 60,000 tonnes of iron ore annually which was only surpassed by the New Tagil mines in the Urals. Production of pig iron was over 28,000 tonnes which was almost double the next largest iron works, though this was only a small proportion of Russia's significantly increased annual output of 500,000 tonnes from over 120 foundries. But by 1898 the new

Russia Company was the country's largest single producer of pig iron. Hughes' annual steel production was relatively more significant, having now risen to over 20,000 tonnes – around 16% of domestic output. The importance of the New Russia Company at this time was commented on by a young radical studying Russian capitalism. Following a tour of the Donbass, V I Lenin noted that *'Iuzovka's industry produced twice as much as all 63 industrial enterprises of Ekaterinoslav, and employed twice as many workers'.* [23]

The company participated in several major exhibitions in Russia and Europe, winning awards in 1882 at the All Russia Exhibition, in 1896 at the Nizhny Novgorod Exposition and in 1900 it won the Grand Prix award at the World Exhibition in Paris. The award in 1896 was in recognition of the pre-eminent position in the industry held by the New Russia Company at that time. It was a citation for excellence in developing steel production, for the production of high quality steel rails, for large-scale development of the coal industry plus its coal mining and extraction systems using compressed air and ventilation of the mine galleries to remove explosive gases. In addition, the quality of the company's housing for its workers was also recognised. John Hughes could not have been happier had he still been alive to see such a comprehensive recognition of the company's achievements! The company's exhibition stand was a very ornate affair in the style of a Greek temple with wrought iron fluted columns, very much in keeping with late Victorian decorative design. The stand included displays of the company's products plus photos of the mines and works. The company produced a special illustrated booklet for the fair with descriptions of its production capabilities and photos of both the works and the town's attractions such as the boating lake. Several groups of workers were selected on the basis of exemplary work records to attend the fair for two weeks at a time. There were later claims that some of these workers were contacted during their visit

23 Theodore Friedgut – ibid

by revolutionaries in Nizhny Novgorod and they brought back illegal literature to Hughesovka.[24]

In the mid 19th century, the Nizhny Novgorod Fair was the largest commercial fair in Russia and possibly the whole world. Held in July and August each year, it attracted industrial and agricultural merchants from across Russia and overseas. Although it later lost ground to other fairs, especially in Moscow and Kharkov, it remained a major event and was regularly attended by the New Russia Company.

The depression of the 1880s and the resultant over-capacity led the iron and steel makers in Russia to form a syndicate to share orders and try to maintain prices. The government was actively involved in supporting this arrangement despite some understandable domestic criticism. Despite the downturn, the New Russia Company continued to invest in its facilities and production capability. More rail track was laid in the works and by 1890 it had seven steam locomotives in operation. This number was steadily increased so that by 1910 46 locomotives were on site, most imported from Britain. At its peak in the 1890s, the company's financial position was excellent. Its balance sheet showed further growth in its assets and more than 50% of the company's assets were in the form of cash, accounts receivable or stock. Although overall profit margins were declining, this left ample room for both further investment as well as continuing high future dividends. Up to the end of the 19th century, the New Russia Company paid between 3% and 5% tax on its profits. The Russian corporate tax system was a flat rate, set annually by the government to meet its budget requirements. This changed in 1899 to a fixed rate that steadily rose during the 20th century with marginal rates reaching 24%. As the number of

---

24   Theodore Friedgut – ibid

enterprises in the Ukraine grew in the late 19th and early 20th centuries, the high early returns declined, despite significant growth in demand. With increased capacity and efficiency, market prices followed a general downward trend. Many companies then tried to further improve efficiency with new technology in a competitive battle to reduce costs or improve quality. This required new capital investment which in turn made it ever more difficult for some companies to declare a good dividend. Everyone had to run very hard to keep up. A few companies did very well, especially those like the New Russia Company that benefited from government contracts but the others mainly just struggled along.

There is no doubt that an important element in Hughes' initial business development strategy was to retain and then re-invest profits in expanding and improving the company's capabilities. This partly explains the lack of dividends in the early years, despite good profits. Even though Hughes was a substantial investor in the company, there were to be no short-term gains for the shareholders. This prudent policy meant no external debt burden or interest costs putting the company in a strong position to ride out the periodic economic crises that Hughes knew would occur. The characteristics of foresight and self-reliance were evident from the very start in the way that Hughes developed and managed the company. Whether it was bringing with him all the necessary men and equipment to build the first works, the location of the town, training his own labour force, having his own rail links or securing adequate supplies of coal and iron to meet expanding production, Hughes planned ahead and did his best to minimise reliance on outsiders. It was not until the end of the 19th century and the renewed expansion of the company by his sons that any significant debt was incurred. In 1898 and 1899, the company floated two 20-year bond issues amounting to £300,000 and then in 1910 a further issue raising £600,000 was made, at the same time pying off the previous bonds ahead of schedule. Alfred Lyttleton MP (see page 165) was one of the trustees for these new bonds which were secured against the company's land holdings. He was a barrister, privy councillor and secretary of state for the British Colonies from 1903 to 1905. In the period from 1903 to 1912 some nine million roubles were invested in the company – dramatic evidence of belief in its future by the shareholders and board. The New Russia Company's shares were never listed on the British stock exchange and the growth in the number of shareholders was simply by invitation to selected British and Russian friends and business contacts (although one investor from the USA is recorded – Albert Revillon of Baltimore).

Albert Revillon married Julia Whistler, the niece of James Whistler, the famous American painter. They lived in St Petersburg for a while in the late 1880s and early 1890s and probably found out about the New Russia Company through meeting Hughes or his son John James there. Julia tried to sell one of Whistler's well-known paintings, The Music Room, in St Petersburg at this time, much to the annoyance of Whistler. The painting was finally sold later at auction in London.

As the business continued to expand and the town grew, the company came up against local vested interests. There were frequent confrontations between the New Russia Company and the Ekaterinoslav administration over taxation issues and the provision of services. Local landowners, who were the traditional political and economic power in the region, wanted the New Russia Company to pay higher local taxes (which would of course reduce the amount they paid). The company was already paying for just about all the services and facilities in Hughesovka and by 1900, it was also paying around £10,000 annually in local taxes in addition to its state taxes of 10% on profits[25]. The company rightly felt that the regional administration was not providing much by way

---

25   Sir Henry Norman – ibid

of return. There was also probably some resentment among other land owners of the success of Hughes' company and especially its impact on local labour availability and wages. This situation may partly explain why Hughesovka was never given the civil status of a town until after the revolution. However, on the few occasions when this subject was raised, the company was clearly against any change in the status quo. This position was compounded by a distinct lack of interest on the part of the Tsarist state in developing local civic institutions and self-government. In 1913, when there was a move in Hughesovka, led mainly by the Jewish merchants to obtain municipal status, the company wrote *'the settlement can have no independent vitality. It exists only as long as the factory and mines of the New Russia Company function'* and also stated *'the company has no intention of giving up any of its land holdings or rights'*.[26] Without any significant external support, the company's intractable position prevailed and the virtual exclusion of the population from any civic role resulted in a fragmented and politically naive community.

The approach Hughes took to running the company and works (and that subsequently followed by his sons) was very much in the Victorian style of a paternalistic employer. He was known as 'the governor' by his British employees but this was more out of fondness than deference. In a difficult environment the provisions he made for the welfare, safety, housing, education and recreation of his workers were among the best in Russia at the time and met or exceeded Russian industrial regulations. He took a keen interest in his workers and their families and would visit them in their homes. He helped to find jobs for their children, either with his company or in Britain and the company would try to find suitable work for widows and injured or older workers.

---

26   Theodore Friedgut – ibid

Ekaterinoslav was a major centre of the Mennonites in Russia prior to the Bolshevik revolution. The Russian Mennonites were descended from Dutch and German Anabaptists who came to south Russia in the late 18th century after Catherine the Great invited all Europeans to come and settle in the area following its recent acquisition from the Ottoman Empire. Seeking religious freedom and exemption from military service, the Mennonites established colonies in the region, becoming very successful farmers. When the Russian government announced a plan in 1870 to end all special minority privileges, the Mennonites, alarmed at the possibility of losing their exemption from military service and the potential loss of their cultural and religious life, started to emigrate to Canada and USA. Realising that 40,000 of Russia's most industrious farmers were preparing to leave for North America, the Russian government sent General Todleben to negotiate with the Mennonites in 1874. He exaggerated the difficulties they would encounter in North America and offered a four-year forestry service programme for men instead of military service. As a result some 30,000 of the Mennonites stayed in south Russia. But after the Bolshevik revolution, many of them were dispossessed and ultimately their remaining properties and possessions were nationalised by the Soviet authorities and religious freedoms were restricted. Most of the Mennonites then decided to leave Russia, with over 20,000 emigrating to Canada and others to Paraguay, Argentina, the USA and Brazil. For those that stayed, life became increasingly difficult under the Soviets and many were exiled to Siberia and other remote regions east of the Urals.

CHAPTER SIX
Labour Relations and Working Conditions

Although the general levels of literacy in Russia were comparable with Europe or the USA at this time, there were distinct skill shortages throughout the country, especially in the newly developing manufacturing sectors. Even though the peasant population was expanding rapidly, outside of the Urals, St Petersburg and Moscow, few had any experience of working in factories or mines. As we have already seen, Hughes realised from very early on that not only would the majority of his workers have to come from outside the Donbass but they would need more training and supervision than would have been the case in Britain. The issue of labour training, productivity and costs was therefore to become increasingly important for Hughes and the other industrialists who were to follow him later into the Donbass. As in Hughesovka, companies found that to both attract and then retain labour, they had to be more pro-active in providing education and on-the-job training. Management was forced to recruit a higher ratio of supervisory staff (when they could find them) and introduce more process checks to maintain quality and reduce wastage. The relatively low quality of the workforce meant that output of machines in Russia was usually lower than that from the same equipment used in similar operations in Europe or the USA. Overall labour productivity was also generally lower, due to both the itinerant nature of the workforce and the greater amount of holidays. All Russian workers were entitled to a large number of religious and official holidays – potentially as many as 36 annually and the average working year in the Donbass was only around 250 days, compared with 278 days in Britain and over 300 days in the USA. Generally, offers of extra pay to work on Sundays or holidays at times of peak demand were met with a refusal by Russian workers. One of the British workers writing home in April 1889 commented on the fact that the Russian employees had just enjoyed 16 days of holiday that Easter when the company had been very busy. As a result, the Russians' average number of working days per month at the New Russia Company was considerably lower than the British employees and these additional labour costs more than offset the lower wage costs of local workers. Hughes later recognised that in many ways it would have been better to employ more skilled workers from abroad but he had promised the government to train local Russian workers and he also understood the potential for increased conflict if he did so. Not all foreign companies followed his approach to training Russians, and the subject of differences in pay and conditions between the two groups of workers was to become a serious issue in the Donbass leading to discontent and strikes by the Russians.

The problems caused by the large number of Russian holidays were remarked on by many contemporary foreign visitors as well as businessmen. *'An immense loss is inflicted by the holidays that occur in summer ... they frequently leave their work for a week at a time ... some priests invent holidays, without, however, performing divine service on such days, when the peasants suspend their work and take to the bottle.*[27] This issue eventually led a frustrated Hughes to take direct action and the story provides an amusing insight into his determination, negotiating skill and his humour. He carefully cultivated a friendship with the local Orthodox bishop and once

---

27   HS Edwards – Russians at Home and Abroad, 1879

he felt the time was right, Hughes made him a proposal after a substantial genial dinner. He explained to the bishop that *'for the success of the new enterprise, so vital to the State, so advantageous to the people, it was absolutely necessary to increase the number of working days. Unfortunately, this could only be done by docking the Orthodox hierarchy in Heaven of some of their rights on earth.*[28]' Hughes went on to explain that there were so many Saints days that surely some were more important than others to the church so would it not be possible to delete a few of the less important ones? In return, by way of compensation, Hughes offered to pay to the Orthodox church, in the person of his reverence, an amount per pud on all the extra iron or steel produced as a result of this concession. *'The proposal was favourably met. The Calendar was sent for, and Welsh ex-miner and Orthodox priest went carefully through it, retaining all names of importance, striking out those of least significance, till in the end John Hughes had gained 10 or 15 per cent, of working days in the year.'*[29] How this substantial new income was to be split between the bishop and his church was left for the bishop's conscience to determine.

It was Hughes' firm intention from the very beginning to employ and train a local workforce as far as possible. He undoubtedly underestimated the time it would take and the problems involved but his longer-term goal was clear and he remained committed to it. The early push by Hughes to both train local workers and raise their skill levels, coupled with his use of modern production techniques in both the mines and factory meant that the ratio of unskilled manual workers to skilled at the New Russia Company was lower than elsewhere. In the latter part of the 19th century there was considerable progress in improving technical education at some Russian universities and colleges, largely as a result of pressure from Ukrainian industrialists. This gradually expanded the

28   John Baddeley – ibid

29   John Baddeley – ibid

pool of Russian technical graduates and with more foreign companies providing on-the-job training, the supply of capable Russian managers and foremen increased significantly. By then, the New Russia Company was already employing several Russians in key positions. Many of this new wave of technical managers went on to become successful entrepreneurs themselves, particularly in south Russia, and played a leading role in the development of the coal and steel industries in the 20th century.

Russian labour laws at the time of Hughes' arrival were not too dissimilar from those in Britain. The factory and mines acts of the 1840s stipulated no children under ten or women could work in mines and the hours of work were limited to ten hours per day. In 1861 the government went further, raising the minimum age for children to 12 with a maximum working day of eight hours for those under 15 and requiring those between 12 and 18 to have their parents' consent to work. Also children under 15 were not allowed to work underground or at night. However, as with many other laws in Russia, neither the limit on the working day nor the rules on employing children were totally adhered to. Throughout most of the 19th century, Donbass factories and mines typically worked shifts of 12 hours. This was certainly the case at the New Russia Company initially and allowed both the mines and the works to operate 24 hours a day, although working hours were reduced at times of recession. By the 20th century, following legislation introduced in 1897 to limit the working day in factories to 11.5 hours, the system had changed considerably and eight-hour shifts had become the norm though senior skilled workers often worked longer, including Hughes' British employees who were usually under contract to work 12-hour shifts for six days per week. However, these shorter shifts were not always to the liking of the Russian workers whose income was effectively reduced. The pressure on incomes also encouraged the employment of children with both parents (who needed the extra money) and mine owners turning a blind eye to the rules. In fact with the increasing demand for coal in the 20th century coupled with the ongoing shortage of miners, the percentage of child workers actually rose so that by 1913 *'there were close to 15,000 children under the age of fifteen among the 168,400 coal miners of the Donbass'*.[30] Further increases in the numbers of women and children employed occurred during the First World War when the government revised the labour laws to ease labour shortages, allowing women and children to work night shifts.

Where possible, parents preferred factory work for their children as it was safer and there were better opportunities to learn a trade with some companies offering apprenticeships. This may have been one of the factors that encouraged peasant families to settle in Hughesovka since the town offered both mining and factory work. Trotsky, when referring to the detrimental impact of capitalism on the Russian peasant, used the phrase *'snatched from the plough and hurled into the factory furnace'* and undoubtedly life was very hard for those families and children that worked in the mines or factories. But perversely Trotsky's phrase simply underlines the realities of Russian life at that time; in the villages most peasant children would start work as soon as they were physically able. So those who came to work in towns like Hughesovka were only swapping one form of labour for another and the extra kopeks a child might earn could make an important difference to an urban family's living standards. The New Russia Company certainly employed children in both its mines and factories though the numbers seem to have been relatively very small, probably never much more than around 100. It is unclear whether this low number was due to Hughes' feelings on the matter from his earlier personal experiences in Britain or a more deep-seated desire to raise the quality of life for children in 'his' town.

The risks to life and limbs were considerable in both the mines and factories, especially for the many transient inexperienced workers.

---

30   Theodore Friedgut – ibid

A moment's carelessness, fatigue or simply bad luck could lead to serious injury or death. Comparisons of coal mining fatalities in Russia versus Britain show that the latter's rate was consistently half that in Russia. Greater mechanisation, better safety procedures and more experienced workers are the main explanations for this. There were also risks to general health from inhalation of coal dust or the fumes in the foundries and in winter, the situation was even worse. Perspiring workers emerging from the warm, humid coal or iron mines at the end of their shift had to trudge home in bitter cold. Those in the rolling mills had to contend with the immense temperatures around the furnaces but were hit just a few feet away by blasts of icy wind blowing through the vast half-open shed-like buildings. Rees Richards a blast furnace manager from Dowlais in South Wales wrote home, '*I have seen 60 degrees of frost here and puddlers working at the furnaces with gloves on and sheepskin coats on their backs.*'[31] With conditions like these, it is not surprising that labour turnover was high and many peasants preferred to hang on to their traditional rural way of life. The safety record at the New Russia Company in both the mines and works was generally much better than that of other companies in the Donbass, especially for fatalities, which ran at around 50% lower. The reasons for this were the better supervision and higher skill levels (due to training) of the company's workers, more safety equipment plus the lower rate of labour turnover ensuring employees were more experienced in their work. The New Russia Company's mines were virtually alone in the Donbass in having good ventilation, reinforced shafts and emergency exits.

The problems experienced by their workers were not entirely lost on the employers and the Congress of Mining Industrialists set up a compensation fund in the mid-1880s to provide benefits following death or injury at work. It took ten years of argument to reach this stage but even then payments by the fund turned out to be

---

31 Susan Edwards – Hughesovka, 1992

slow and inadequate. As a result, Hughes, along with several other companies, stayed out of the system, preferring to pay more generous benefits themselves. At the New Russia Company married workers that were injured or ill received full pay for the duration of their incapacity and single workers were paid half their wage. In addition the company tried to find suitable work for widows and injured employees and in the 20th century set up a weaving shop and a shoe making shop for just this purpose, both making a wide range of goods for use in the works as well as the town at large. These two facilities illustrate the company's humane approach to its workers and in line with Hughes' view that *'earned money was inherently superior to even the most humanitarian of charities, the New Russia management found a way to accommodate conscience, principle, and thrifty economics all within the social framework of Hughesovka'.*[32] In 1904 the government introduced new legislation to significantly improve the payment of worker death and injury benefits which finally forced the Congress to adopt a more generous system including a new insurance fund.

The Russian government had passed a law in 1866 requiring that all industrial and mining companies provide healthcare for all employees. This was to be free for all work-related injuries and illness but charges could be made for all other cases. Once again this law was largely ignored with companies either claiming they could not afford such provisions or stating, with some justification, that it was the responsibility of the local civil administration to organise and fund medical care for the whole population, including workers. Although companies could not openly go against the law, many simply put in place a bare minimum healthcare system. In the Donbass, this standoff between industrialists and local officials ran deeper than arguments about medical provision. It reflected a growing power struggle between business owners and the existing ruling elite concerning representation and the amount and usage

---

32 Theodore Friedgut – ibid

of local taxes. It related not only to healthcare but to the wider provision of services for the burgeoning population of the region, including education and general welfare. This was a problem Hughes and later his son were to periodically encounter in their dealings with the local officials in Ekaterinoslav and resulted in regular friction between them.

The Russian government tried to reinforce and clarify the situation with the 1886 law on working conditions which made it illegal to take payments from employees for healthcare. But still a large number of companies, especially in mining, remained reactive rather than proactive. Where provisions were made, the medical facilities were generally only sufficient for day-to-day accidents and totally inadequate for serious illness or outbreaks of infectious diseases. At the time of the famine and cholera outbreak in 1892 according to a government report, more than half of the Donbass mines had no medical facilities whatsoever and there were only 11 hospitals in the region. These had to serve a population of around 1.4 million people working in some 500 mines, factories and industrial plants.

When Hughes arrived in the Donbass in 1870, he would have been aware of the 1866 law regarding healthcare and the company's first 12-bed hospital was in fact constructed in the very first year, before the works were actually in operation. Thus it was clear from the outset that Hughes placed great importance on the health of his employees as well as the general population of Hughesovka. All workers at the new Russia Company were entitled to medical care and medicines were free. Bath houses for the miners were also provided free of charge. A pharmacy was added in 1874 as well as a sanitary commission to inspect foodstuffs and the hospital and medical facilities were gradually expanded to try to cope with growing needs. Of course, the numbers of beds, doctors and nurses were never enough to fully cope with the steady rise in the number of workers and the overall population of the town. However, in the

19th century the New Russia Company was way ahead of other companies in the size and quality of its healthcare services and it seems that this fact was recognised on several occasions by government officials. Following a visit to Hughesovka, one inspector wrote, *'The ordinary and extraordinary were being accomplished and nothing was left to be desired as arrangements far surpassed those at other mines in the district.*[33] In 1893 the company's facilities included a gynaecological ward, a surgical ward plus an isolation ward and the annual cost to the company of providing the medical services was close to 45,000 roubles. By 1901 the cost of this service had grown more than three times to over 150,000 roubles and as yet, there were still no permanent healthcare facilities provided by the local administration. In the 20th century the company's own medical provisions were also gradually supplemented by doctors working in private practices. Despite the high levels of taxes paid by the New Russia Company and other enterprises in the area, there was a marked lack of help and support on the part of local government, even during periods of major crisis when outbreaks of typhus, smallpox and cholera occurred. Indeed it seems that local officials at times even discouraged expansion of medical services by blocking doctors' suggestions and applications for improvements. This disgraceful situation continued until 1911 when the first non-company hospital was built in Hughesovka, some 40 years after the start of the settlement.

Any discussion of healthcare arrangements in the town inevitably also has to include a look at the prevailing water and sanitary conditions. The town was regularly criticised by residents, government officials and visitors for its unhealthy conditions and overall lack of basic hygiene. Fundamental to this situation was the scarcity of water in the region, which had always been one of the contributory factors limiting its population growth. The majority of settlements in the Donbass relied on wells for their drinking water but the

---

33   Theodore Friedgut – ibid

quality of water from these was usually poor and sometimes polluted due to their proximity to industrial and mining activities. In Hughesovka the damming of the Kalmius river by the company in the late 1880s improved the situation there, supplementing two other existing reservoirs and local wells. But one of these reservoirs caught all local surface water runoff, including that from the works and town so without any treatment facility, could only be used for the works and fire station. For almost all its drinking water the town depended on 12 stone-built wells that were permanently guarded by watchmen provided by the company, usually injured workers from the mines or factory. The water was sent to holding tanks by steam-driven pumps from where it was distributed through the town by a variety of private and company water carriers. Such a system was inevitably a contributor to health problems caused by water-born diseases, especially in the hot dry summer months. This relatively primitive process remained in operation until 1915 when a closed pipe water and sewage system was built by the company.

Water shortages also contributed to the limited number of baths taken by people in the town, especially amongst the miners, which in turn lowered personal hygiene standards. As well as bathing facilities in the workers' housing, the company provided baths for the factory and mines and in the 20th century there were commercial baths as well as a Jewish public bath. Although these facilities were inadequate to fully cope with the whole population, there also appears to have been a strange lack of either desire or understanding of the need for regular bathing, especially among the itinerant Donbass peasant miners. Sadly, the attitude towards dirt and hygiene by some sections of the community seems to have been one of acceptance as being a part of life in the town. The situation was compounded throughout the Donbass by problems relating to the removal of garbage and human waste. In theory the doctors were responsible for inspecting the works and mines for unsanitary conditions but although they made recommendations for change, these were largely ignored by their employers, the company owners. In Hughesovka the position was somewhat better, due initially to Hughes' awareness of the problems and dangers from his earlier life in South Wales. He fully understood that improved hygiene would not come from his actions alone or simply by issuing rules for the factory and mines. From very early days, he had established a sanitary commission for the town and this continued in operation throughout the period of the New Russia Company's existence. However, until the cholera outbreak of 1892, the steps taken to remove garbage and human waste in public areas were minimal. Subsequently there was a step change in activity; all houses were built with an outhouse in the yard, a new garbage dump was created, waste was removed daily by wagons, outhouses were installed at the works and mines with hermetically sealed containers placed in the mine tunnels and a public health officer was recruited. Impressive though this list is, it took time to implement these initiatives and not all sections of the community benefited, with inevitably the poorer districts lagging behind. The amounts spent by the company on this problem were still small compared with other elements of its budget and not all the actions undertaken were as effective as they might have been. The waste wagons leaked badly leaving a trail of residue in the streets and the first garbage dump was badly located. In addition, despite the measures put in place, some residents continued to use their yards, the streets or nearby spare ground as a dump for garbage and waste. As with the attitude to bathing mentioned above, there seems to have been a lack of interest in taking individual responsibility for providing a clean, healthy environment. Given Hughes' specific previous experience of cholera outbreaks in Merthyr due to poor sanitation, it is hard to understand why he (or subsequently his sons) did not do more to improve arrangements in the town. This was not something that could be left to the individual residents to effect improvement. It was not that he was uncaring or disinterested. In fact in 1879 when there was a cholera outbreak in the Donbass, he wrote to the government –

'Ever since I have been in south Russia I have impressed on the work-men in our employ to abstain from drinking vodka as much as possible and also to avoid eating a large amount of cucumbers and melons and especially unripe fruit. I have also impressed upon our doctors as also on our police to look after the cleanliness and ventilation of the houses as well as the people themselves, as all doctors agree that cleanliness is the enemy of diseases.'[34]

Doctor Goldgardt who ran the company hospital for over 20 years worked closely with Hughes and his sons to try to improve living conditions in Hughesovka. Almost certainly he would not have stayed so long if he had felt he was not listened to or progress was not being made. During the first major Donbass cholera outbreak in 1892, many people evacuated the town causing disruption to production and general commercial activity. Families of many British workers returned home for several months until the all-clear and it is estimated that some 40,000 people fled the Donbass during the cholera epidemic of 1910. There was thus a measurable cost to such epidemics for the company as well as more indirect impacts on the town and community. Of course Hughes was not alone in failing to take adequate steps to provide good sanitation; his fellow industrialists and the local administrators did even less. Cholera and typhus epidemics also affected other towns across Russia, including St Petersburg in the 19th and 20th centuries; over one million people died in the first outbreak in 1860, 90,000 in 1866 and close to 270,000 in 1892. So Hughesovka was not unique in failing to adequately deal with this serious threat to public health and by the standards of the day was no worse in this respect than most other Russian towns. However, Hughes and his sons had the experience, power and capability to do more and of all the criticisms levelled at the New Russia Company, this is probably the one that is most justified. Having taken the lead in so many things, Hughes' lack of timely action in this respect is out of character.

---

34 Theodore Friedgut – ibid

The wage rates of locally hired workers varied according to labour supply and the rise and fall of production over economic cycles. In the early years, Hughes' miners earned from 22 to 28 roubles per month and highly skilled factory workers up to 60 roubles based on a typical working month of 20 days plus a free coal allowance. As a comparison, monthly wage rates at the government's Alexandrovsk locomotive works in St Petersburg in the 1860s were around 35 roubles for a master mechanic and 20 roubles for a skilled foreman. The typical *annual* wage for a hired agricultural worker at the time was only 70 roubles. Although the wages of Hughes' workers were considerably higher than agricultural workers, their cost of living and working was also greater, mostly due to rents and food. However, they generally enjoyed a better diet, consuming much more meat, cabbage, potatoes and wheat flour than rural workers who rarely had such luxuries to eat. Also bribery was pernicious in Russia with workers having to pay their supervisors for better positions or to overlook minor transgressions and this took a share of wages. Hughes attempted to stamp out this practice at the New Russia Company but it proved impossible to fully eliminate. In the early years, Hughes tried a strict piecework pay system for both British and Russian workers to try to encourage higher productivity but this proved unpopular with many of his employees and he later introduced more flexibility. By the 1890s Hughesovka's unskilled factory workers and miners were earning 28 to 30 roubles per month, almost double the average Russian factory worker's monthly wage in Russia at the time of 17 roubles. The best skilled workers earned up to 100 roubles per month and the differential continued to widen up to the time of the First World War. The New Russia Company's pay rates were not only significantly higher than prevailing rates elsewhere in Russia, they were also ten to 15% higher than at other companies in the Donbass which not only helped attract workers but also meant that they felt better about their work and life generally in Hughesovka. Fines were imposed universally by Russian companies for infractions of their rules such as unauthorised absence or arriving late for a shift. The money raised from the fines usually went to the company but Hughes set up a workers' committee to use the fines for workers' welfare. It was typical of the man that he introduced a more benevolent approach and was one of the few examples of genuine worker involvement in any aspect of a company in Russia at this time. It is no surprise that much of the later labour militancy in the Donbass emanated from outside of Hughesovka.

The typical pay rate for the first group of British workers that Hughes brought with him was £10 or 80 roubles per month and this gradually increased during the 19th century. This was some ten to 15% more than comparable skilled workers were earning at the time in London. In addition, for the British skilled workers in Hughesovka with subsidised housing, free coal and cheap food, their living costs were less than half those in Britain. Hughes had little choice in importing British skilled workers initially but as production grew there were periodic debates in the company about the use of British workers versus locals. The British cost more to employ but were more productive, working longer hours each month and didn't need training as they were already familiar with the technology in use. But Hughes was fully aware of the potential tensions if too many foreign workers were brought in. As the supply of skilled local workers rose in the 20th century the wage differentials between Russian and foreign skilled workers steadily narrowed so that by 1914 pay rates were similar which helped to ease the problem. John Hughes' initial annual salary was £1,000, which was a very attractive wage for the time but actually significantly lower than the salaries of some other foreign managers in Russia. In the latter part of the 19th century, expatriate directors in foreign-owned steel companies typically received two or three times this amount with some earning over £4,000 annually. Chief engineers could expect £900 to £1,000 and even inexperienced technical graduates were paid over £450. In 1914 the company's Russian general manager was paid 40,000 roubles per year, equivalent to about £4,000 at the time. As the number of foreign companies in Russia rose, competition for good managers increased and inevitably some less capable men were employed – at least until their short-comings were discovered! Work in southern Russia at the time was for determined, capable, tough-minded men and it took a special blend of talent and energy to succeed. Also it could be dangerous, especially into the 20th century with increasing worker unrest; several foreign managers were assassinated and others forced to flee the country at times of severe disturbances. Reputations were won or lost quickly but with low living costs and little to spend money on locally, the successful manager could hope to earn a small fortune by the end of a good contract.

All commercial transactions in Hughesovka were in cash as the New Russia Company did not operate any truck shops or credit systems, unlike many other companies across Russia. Prices in company stores were regularly 20% to 100% higher than in local markets and so this made a big difference to workers' disposable incomes. Despite being outlawed in 1886, the practice of payment in kind or by coupons redeemable at the company store continued for many years in Russia. Payment of wages was only made twice a year in the early days of Donbass industry, usually at Easter and in October, when wage rates were also reviewed. From the companies' viewpoint, there was some logic to this as the extended period between payments helped tie the worker to the enterprise. The factory act of 1886 required payment of wages twice monthly but as with so many laws, it was largely ignored for many years. However, in 1887, the New Russia Company agreed to introduce monthly payments for all employees, although they insisted that everyone should work two weeks in hand to try to prevent workers leaving without notice. The wages were brought from the bank in Taganrog under armed escort until a bank was established in Hughesovka at the turn of the century. The amount of cash involved was very considerable, with a monthly payroll around £5,000 (over £500,000 in today's values but equivalent to £2.5 million if adjusted for the growth in average earnings). The company was criticised in 1900 by

118

government inspectors for only paying monthly and holding back two weeks' pay but it was a major improvement on the methods in operation at most other companies in the region.

Taganrog was one of the largest industrial cities in southern Russia at the beginning of the 20th century, dominated by the Belgian-owned iron and steel works established in 1896 and was the second largest port in Russia handling imported goods. It is also famous as the birthplace of the Russian author Chekov and where in 1833 the Italian Garibaldi joined the 'Young Italy' society that took him on his later campaign to liberate Italy from Austrian rule.

As has already been described, recruiting and retaining labour was one of the most significant problems faced by Hughes and his company and in this respect the provision of housing was to become a key factor. Since nothing was available at the site on the empty steppe selected for building the works, one of the early priorities was to construct accommodation in order to be able to attract workers from Britain or within Russia. For his senior British employees, Hughes recognised he had to match standards at home so he built good quality stone and brick houses. The Russian factory workers were initially provided with smaller stone houses clustered around the works but as the labour force expanded, brick and wooden buildings were constructed. These were also used for the growing number of Russian traders, shopkeepers and other new arrivals seeking work outside the company. However, most unskilled labourers and miners had to accept a far lower standard of accommodation. Although by the mid-1800s, wooden dormitories and barracks were being built by some mine and factory owners, transient peasant workers in Russia traditionally depended on the 'dug-out' which they constructed themselves. This system was prevalent throughout the country outside the main cities but these living conditions were very harsh and amenities very limited, hardly suitable for families. The dug-out in typical use in the Donbass was not much more than a shallow trench, lined with stones or boards. Small walls were constructed from earth or mine residue, a simple wooden structure supported an earthen roof and a low door provided air and light. Windows were rare and the floor was simply bare earth. Single men slept on tiered plank sleeping shelves with up to 50 to a room. Families would be allocated one room, regardless of their size and everyone shared a single communal kitchen and coal stove. The dug-out was never expected to be a permanent home as most of these itinerant workers intended to return to their villages after a few months' work. It suited the temporary nature of much of the work in the forests and mines, which were generally sited away from the towns and villages. It also had the basic advantages of being quick and cheap to construct from the materials readily to hand and could be easily adapted to changing numbers of occupants. The problem in the Donbass was that due to the region's housing shortage, these dug-outs increasingly became longer-term accommodation for a growing number of workers who had no alternative to these grim and unhealthy conditions.

Hughes understood that if he was to attract Russian workers and persuade them to settle in Hughesovka to form a permanent workforce, he would need more than dug-outs. His approach was to try to build sufficient company dormitories and housing to accommodate all his workers from the very start. This policy eased the immediate labour recruitment problem but initially did little to encourage workers and their families to settle and move away from their traditional seasonal pattern of returning to their villages. However, with time, regular wages, decent housing plus an expanding settlement providing amenities such as shops and a social life, the company's employees gradually became residents rather than temporary workers. By the early 1880s, Hughes had built sufficient accommodation for 4,000 people and had all but eradicated the 'dug-out'. But then Hughes' attitude seems to change, appearing contradictory and with the rapidly increasing numbers of mine workers at the company plus the rising population of the town in general, the New Russia Company failed to keep up with demand for housing. Unskilled labour was now plentiful and cheap and Hughes seems to have held the view that anything would do for them and so for a time less priority was given to building housing for miners and labourers. As their numbers continued to rise, the pressure on available accommodation, usually company barracks, intensified, leading to overcrowding and miserable conditions. Also as the need for more coal grew, the location of new mines moved further away from the towns and villages to more isolated areas where there was little or no housing. In rural areas, local Ukrainian peasants were reluctant to rent space in their homes to these dirty, itinerant workers from outside the Donbass who were threatening their traditional ways of life. This forced many of the miners to fall back on the 'dug-out', despite a government decree in 1894 requiring that all 'dug-outs' should cease to be used within two years. During the 1900s government surveys regularly pointed out the dreadful conditions of many mining communities in the Donbass region but little was done to change things. The unhealthy lifestyle, disease and social depredation for many of the miners and their families continued well into the 1920s. Although the conditions for many miners at the New Russia Company were undoubtedly poor, in general their situation was significantly better than elsewhere in the Donbass.

The majority of factory workers were still able to find accommodation in the town, either building their own home or renting. The private rental sector was becoming increasingly important as a source of accommodation in Hughesovka and in the 20th century the percentage of workers in company housing was falling, averaging around only 30%. The rising demand for housing was also partly met through the sub-letting of rooms in apartments and by company employees with houses erecting sheds in their

121

gardens for rent. All this was strictly against company rules forbidding employees to take in guests in company accommodation with the threat of a fine of three days' wages. Typically Hughes did not want to see increased overcrowding and health problems among workers in company housing. But mounting housing pressures in the town and the desire for extra income meant this rule was often ignored. In 1912 there was an average of almost 13 people in each dwelling in Hughesovka, which was high by Russian provincial town standards of the time but comparable to other growing industrial towns in the Donbass and certainly well below some of the levels in major industrial centres of Europe. The type and quality of housing provided by the company in the town varied considerably over the years. A two-roomed apartment in Hughesovka with entrance hall plus a stove in each room cost four roubles per month in 1890 which represented about a day's pay for a skilled factory worker and less than a week's pay for the lowest paid workers and miners. More basic single room apartments with a shared kitchen were renting for 1.5 roubles per month. Further up the scale were homes with four large rooms, summer and winter kitchens, all services including heat and water for eight roubles per month – still only two days' pay for a skilled worker. In 1904 in Krivoi Rog, the company was building modern centrally heated barracks with brick walls, cement floors, separate living spaces and wash rooms for its miners. The majority of dwellings in Hughesovka were built from stone and brick with iron roofs. Wooden buildings in the town were less common, unusually for Russia, due to the shortage of wood on the steppe. The Russian peasants that came to live and work in Hughesovka initially tried to follow their traditional rural ways by keeping livestock on the land around their homes. This was partly because it was their way of life and partly due to the rising cost of food in urban Russia. This practice was eventually banned by Hughes on the basis of general hygiene and his desire to see the workers fully urbanised and not return to their migratory ways. This resulted in protests by some of the workers and accusations that the British were trying to impose their own standards in a foreign country. But Hughes prevailed, saying that Hughesovka was a factory town, not the steppe. Although worker retention remained a problem, Hughes' approach saw typical worker contract periods gradually rise from a few months to several years.

By the end of the 19th century, Hughes had provided sufficient housing for almost all the company's factory workers and their families plus a high percentage of the miners. Hughes was the first to achieve this level of provision of worker housing and the first to offer a comprehensive package of barracks, apartments and houses to rent or buy. This enlightened approach placed the New Russia Company in an advantageous position versus its local competitors whose workers had less choice and were not nearly as settled. But this benefit came at a significant cost. We have no detailed yearly records for Hughes' company that show the exact annual amounts spent on building and maintaining these dwellings. However, information drawn from other Donbass company records and government surveys indicates construction costs ranging from around 80 roubles for single workers to 800 roubles for families, depending on location, overall size and quality of the housing unit. In fact the rental cost mentioned above for the two-bed apartment was calculated by the company to yield a 6% return on the building's value which would equate to an 800 rouble build cost. The housing costs for a mine would generally be lower than for a factory due to the higher number of single miners. However, an example recorded for a mine in 1900 where *'together with the costs for a school, hospital ... the outlay on housing was figured at 500,000 roubles'*.[35] This represented 25% of the estimated overall investment required to develop the mine. Using a weighted average figure of 300 roubles for all types of housing, this would indicate an investment by the New Russia Company of 1.8 million roubles (almost £17 million today) for the 6,000 workers shown in company housing in 1900. Services and maintenance charges would have increased this cost

---

35 Theodore Friedgut – ibid

and in addition, the company built and funded schools, hospitals and other social assets. In 1916 the company's accounts showed a book value of 1.5 million roubles for all its housing and commercial property, not including the land, factory or mining assets. We can look at the challenge faced by the New Russia Company another way. In the 20th century the town received an average of over 2,300 new residents each year up to the start of the First World War, despite economic downturns and the 1905 revolution. Using an average unit build cost of 300 roubles and a 30% rate of demand for company housing, the annual investment potentially required by the company simply to meet new demand would have been over 200,000 roubles. This simple example of course ignores several important factors such as increased occupancy levels. These are very significant numbers and partly indicate why the company failed to keep up with demand for housing in the 20th century. Such levels of investment by the company over many years diverted capital away from its primary business purpose, as well as taking up management time to organise and administrate. But the levels of housing investment made by the company clearly illustrate its determination to stabilise the work force as well as a commitment to improving their lot and developing the new town of Hughesovka. Almost regardless of the year, the New Russia Company consistently had a greater percentage of its workers in individual houses and a higher number of workers living with their with families than in any other Donbass settlement.

As we have seen, Hughes built housing, hospitals, churches and schools for his workers in Hughesovka but the New Russia Company was not the only Russian company to provide housing and social assets for its workers. Driven by many of the same labour problems faced by Hughes, there had been a growing trend among larger companies since the middle of the 19th century to provide housing and maintain schools, churches and other social assets in several parts of the country. It has been estimated that these early 'social' capital costs averaged up to 10% of the total wages bill. In the Donbass heavy industrial areas with their need for a greater proportion of company housing in the 20th century, these labour-related costs amounted in some cases *'to 30% of the total overhead expenses for an enterprise'*.[36] But once worker housing was in place, it became a powerful incentive for permanent migration from other regions in Russia, with many workers travelling great distances. It is interesting to read the account of one such worker from Orel province –

'I was earning little and ... worried about it. Finally I decided to go (south) in search of a living... I went on foot – 840 kilometres in 23 days. I left New Year's Day and on the 23rd of January 1884, I arrived at the mine.'[37]

The 1897 census indicated that around 70% of the workers in mining and manufacturing in southern Russia were born in other provinces. In the Donbass area, contemporary estimates put the proportion of immigrant miners even higher at over 85%. Perversely, as Hughesovka steadily grew and its workforce became more settled, the town then became not only a model for other entrepreneurs to emulate but also a source of labour for other mines and factories in southern Russia.

If the need for housing to attract workers was relatively well understood by the end of the 19th century, it was not always successfully implemented, especially by some of the large coal mining companies in the Donbass which as a result often ran short of workers. The issue of worker housing and labour retention remained a frequently debated topic at meetings of the Congress of Mining Industrialists. Part of the explanation lies in the short leases of many coal mining companies which rendered the large investments needed for housing uneconomic. Poor management and the drive for short-term

---

36   William Blackwell – ibid
37   John McKay – ibid

profits also made it difficult to justify these long-term investments. The situation was made worse by the recession of the early 1900s which hit profits severely. Because the New Russia Company had maintained a regular programme of building accommodation from its start in 1870, it had both a large stock of housing and good retained profits so it was in a better position to weather the occasional economic downturns. This sustained house building policy of Hughes and the company also meant that new arrivals in Hughesovka had a better choice of accommodation – company barracks, company rented apartments and houses, land on which to build, houses to buy and private sector housing. Workers' housing plus related social issues have been one of the most discussed issues in the context of industrial expansion in south Russia and the actions of the New Russia Company both at the time and in more recent studies. We will examine this further in the final chapter.

The recruitment of workers from other parts of Russia by the large Donbass companies was often haphazard and irregular through most of the 19th century. However, Hughes was more pro-active and organised in this respect using agents and other contacts to try to bring both skilled and peasant workers in to Hughesovka. There was one other difference between Hughes' approach to labour re-cruitment and that of other Donbass enterprises. Traditionally in Russia, peasants would come from their villages to work in groups called 'cartels' with a leader who would act as the go-between for the workers with company management. They would live and work as a group, essentially acting as contractors. With few exceptions, Hughes preferred not to use such groups in either his mines or works unlike most other companies. He felt that by direct hire and employment he would have more control over both the quality of work as well as building more loyalty to the company and the town. There were also two other categories of labour that became increasingly important in the development of the factories and mines in south Russia in the second half of the 19th century. Firstly, as the rate of foreign investment grew in the region, experienced managers and workers from Lithuania and Poland (then part of Tsarist Russia) were brought in, often from associated companies there. Some were familiar with the technology and methods being introduced into Russia and were not only cheaper to employ than expatriate Belgian, French or German technicians but most also spoke Russian. Secondly, companies in south Russia were willing to employ Jewish workers. The position of the Jews in 19th century Russian social and economic life was difficult and strictly regulated by law. Permanent residence by the Jews was restricted to the Pale of Settlement, an area established by Catherine II and including much of present day Lithuania, Belarus, Poland, Bessarabia, Ukraine and parts of western Russia. They were not generally allowed to live in rural areas and they were prohibited from a number of the major cities within the pale. Only a limited number of categories of Jews were allowed to live outside the pale. There was a reluctance on the part of most Russian managers to employ Jews who were viewed as either not truly Russian or untrustworthy and potentially politically disruptive. However, there was much greater tolerance towards Jews in foreign-owned companies like the New Russia Company. Thus although Jews accounted for less than 5% of the overall population of the Ukraine in the latter part of the 19th century, their numbers were more than double this in the towns of the Donbass including Hughesovka. As trade and industry grew in the region in the 20th century, so did the numbers of Jews, rising in some towns to 20% of the population.

As Hughesovka was not yet officially designated a town, in theory Jews were not allowed to live there and this uncertainty surrounding its status probably held back the growth of the Jewish population in Hughesovka to an extent. The Jews of Hughesovka formed only a small percentage of the New Russia Company's employees, mostly working in administrative, sales or supervisory roles in the company and as a result were not really integrated with either the factory or mine workers. Most were engaged in commerce and trade, which was dominated by the Jewish community. Although this brought them constantly into contact with the rest of the town's population, there was always a dislike and distrust of the Jews which led to violence at times of strikes and riots in the town. Despite these social tensions, the fact that Hughes and the other foreign industrialists who followed him were less constrained by traditional Russian attitudes and happy to employ these two groups gave them an advantage over Russian companies in overcoming labour and skill shortages.

This anti-Jewish sentiment was a reflection of the situation that had existed in Russia generally for many years. After the Jews had been implicated in the assassination of Tsar Alexander II, his successor Alexander III increased the persecution of Jews significantly. In 1886 the Tsar approved laws limiting the number of Jewish pupils in schools of all grades and Jews were forbidden to establish their own schools. From 1887 those living in Russia outside the pale were forced from their homes and made to relocate (in 1890 more than 700 Jews were expelled from Moscow) and Kiev plus parts of the Crimea were excluded from the pale. Jews were not allowed to hold any official office, although they were obliged to serve in the army but unable to rise from the ranks. They could not be employed on the railways or work in their construction. Certain trades were permitted but these were never properly defined and the list of exemptions was frequently and arbitrarily changed. For example, watchmakers were prosecuted because they also sold watch keys and tailors because they did not manufacture the buttons attached on the clothes sold.

Labour unrest in Russia became a growing issue in the last decade of the 19th century, linked both to poor working conditions as well as to the general social malaise affecting the country. Despite the significant improvements to Hughesovka and its quality of life, the town was not immune to the labour unease and suffered from several strikes. The first occurred as early as 1874 when a relatively small percentage of the New Russia Company's coal miners struck over pay and conditions. Hughes had offered the miners a good pay rise but wanted them to sign a three-year contract in return which was not acceptable to many of the miners. The dispute rumbled on for several months eventually turning into open conflict when a few of the miners attempted to occupy the works. They were driven back by a combined group of factory managers and workers and after running fights in the town, some of the miners were captured and handed over to the police. This was the first significant split in Hughesovka between the miners and factory workers that was to increasingly impact labour relations and social cohesion in the town and the Donbass generally. Later the same year there was a minor dispute with a few steel workers brought in from the Lugansk over Hughes' rigid piecework rates. A further strike took place at Easter in 1875 over late payment of wages, this time involving both miners and factory workers and led to some looting of shops and taverns in the town. However, no attacks were made against company property, indicating that the workers had not become vindictive against the company. Hughes claimed he had held back payment of part of the wages so that it would not be wasted on drink during the Easter holiday but the late payment was more likely due to financial problems in the company. The strike and rioting ended after mediation by the company doctor and the regional police chief, resulting in a public statement to the whole workforce by Hughes that the outstanding money would be paid in three days and in future all wages would be paid monthly. Hughes' previous experience of strikes and riots as a young man in Merthyr Tydfil would have made him alert to the dangers of labour strife and helps explain his personal intervention as well as the early company funding for the local police station and Cossack troop.

Clearly in these early instances of labour problems, Hughes had not gained the full measure of his Russian workforce. However, having survived these problems, he quickly learnt to be more flexible and adapt to local conditions, gaining the respect of his workers. Also as the company grew in size and profitability, he had more scope with wage rates, working hours and overtime. Hughes wrote to a government minister in 1879 that his own father's solution to the labour unrest that swept through Britain in the 1830s had been to *give the men plenty of work!* [38] Although there were further periodic disputes, the New Russia Company successfully avoided any further strikes until 1898, unlike other companies in the region. In 1887 when 1,200 miners from the nearby Rutchenko mines went on strike, some came to Hughesovka to seek support and were once more driven out by Hughes' workers, although three people were killed in the struggle. In 1892 during the widespread cholera riots in the Donbass, there was serious disorder in Hughesovka, mostly led by the miners, leading to considerable looting and burning of shops and several people were killed. But when miners from outside Hughesovka tried to attack the factory, they were again driven off by the workers, although not before some damage was done to machinery in the works. In 1898, a two-week strike for shorter working hours resulted in a reduction in the New Russia Company's working day to 10.5 hours. Under Russian law, collective action by strikers could be punished by a term in prison but this action was never implemented in Hughesovka.

The economic downturn at the start of the 20th century caused major labour problems in Russian companies, similar to those affecting other industrialised nations at the time. Strikes, lock-outs, reductions in wages and hours and the formation of labour unions were commonplace. But in Russia, the situation was exacerbated by the heavy-handed, often violent, intervention of the authorities, sometimes using troops to break up strikes. This had the de-stabilising effect of giving the mounting labour unrest across the country an added political protest dimension. With many Donbass workers

---

38   T H Friedgut John Hughes of Iuzovka, 1991

laid off or on short time during the 1900-03 recession stoppages became more common with nine serious strikes. Disruption across south Russia peaked during the 1905 revolution, as leftist agitation provoked considerable labour unrest. Armed workers were repeatedly in confrontations with police, local Cossack forces or regular troops and at the end of the year 1,500 miners were involved in a battle with soldiers in an attempt to seize the Ekaterinin railway line. However in the midst of this chaos, production at the New Russia Company continued with no major stoppages due to labour unrest. The approach of Hughes and later his sons to maintaining good labour relations clearly paid off, allowing the company to benefit from a much better strike record relative to other companies in south Russia at the time. The unusual support of the management by the factory workers during some of the periods of turmoil is a testament to the esteem in which the New Russia Company and the Hughes family were held.

Due to the lack of accurate records, there are inevitably differing estimates of the actual number of workers employed by the New Russia Company but a good guide is provided by Friedgut[39] which is derived from a variety of original Russian sources. Selected numbers from his more detailed tables show the growth rates of both miners and factory workers in relation to Hughesovka's approximate overall population.

Year	Miners	Factory Workers	Total Workers	Population
1871	-	-	451	480
1874	370	1436	1806	2000
1880	-	2000	-	4000
1884	625	2400	3025	5500

---

39 Theodore Friedgut – ibid

Year	Miners	Factory Workers	Total Workers	Population
1890	1773	6326	8099	18000
1897	3975	8807	12782	28000
1901	6226	8925	15151	36000
1907	7095	6340	14435	47000
1913	9935	8045	17980	52500
1916	-	-	20000	70000

The growth in employment was not always continuous and in some years, usually due to the Russian economic situation, the numbers declined. However, the almost ten-fold increase in the number of workers between 1874 (when iron production was first in full spate) and 1913 is impressive. These numbers are significant for several reasons. Firstly, they give a good idea of the challenge that was faced by the company in providing accommodation (plus ancillary services) for such a rapidly growing workforce. Housing for 5,000 new workers and their families was needed over the period 1884 to 1890 and again from 1896 to 1901. Secondly, the figures show the steady rise in the percentage of the population not employed directly by the company. Although many of these were the miners' and workers' dependants, within this change is a rising number of people in the service sector – shopkeepers, merchants, servants, officials etc. As early as 1884 they already accounted for 25% of the population and inevitably their views on the town's development and civic structures would differ from the company and its own employees. Thirdly, this table not only illustrates the increasingly significant number of coal miners employed by the company but also the changing balance between miners and factory workers over the period. This had important impacts on not only labour relations but also Hughesovka society in general. We have already seen that the miners received lower pay and generally poorer housing than the factory workers. As the number of miners increased and then surpassed that of factory workers, this was bound to increase friction in labour relations as well as out in the wider community of the town. By 1913 some 600 New Russia Company workers owned their own homes, virtually all of them factory workers and thousands more rented accommodation that was much superior to that provided for the miners. This increasing disparity between the various groups inevitably led to diverging social and political attitudes in the years leading up to the 1905 and 1917 revolutions.

What is not apparent from the table is both the steadily increasing retention rate of Russian workers and the continuing high percentage of workers from outside the local Ekaterinoslav district. In 1884 it is estimated that over 30% of the total labour force had been with the company for ten years or more and over 70% of Hughes' workers came from regions outside Ekaterinoslav.[40] These figures show the relative early success of his policies in developing a stable workforce at the same time as underlining the continuing problem of finding local labour. By the time of the First World War, the population of Hughesovka had become very much like that of any other normal industrial town, with equal numbers of males and females and a rapidly rising percentage aged under 16. Company town it may have been but it had also developed a diversified economy with a significant service sector providing jobs for women and older men. It was now a family town with a relatively settled population quite unlike much of the rest of the Donbass and Hughes' original concept of a skilled, urbanised workforce had finally taken shape.

---

40   Theodore Friedgut – ibid

CHAPTER SEVEN
Life in Hughesovka

Although there is little information regarding the specific details of the day-to-day life of the Hughes family in Hughesovka, there is a sufficient number of contemporary letters and subsequent recollections to give us a good idea of what life was like for the British and Russian residents. Inevitably, life in the early days was very difficult for the newly arrived group of British workers. Everything around them was unfamiliar; none of them spoke Russian, their accommodation was basic with no amenities, what local food was available was quite different and of course they were alone without their families. Adjusting to the early arrival of an unusually cold winter would also have been hard. But in time as the little settlement grew, conditions improved and like new arrivals in any country, they adapted and learnt to live more comfortably in their new environment, becoming a tight-knit and very sociable group. Not surprisingly, the climatic extremes compared with Britain were one of the things most frequently commented on by the British families. Everything seemed on a much greater scale here – the vast, flat steppe compared with the small, intimate hills and valleys of home, the huge quantities of snow and ice in winter and the morass of mud as the snows melted in the spring, when galoshes were essential footwear. One of the British wives described conditions in her letters home in 1913 '*one could get about the streets in boats if the liquid mud was a little deeper'* and in August *'not a cool spot to be found anywhere, and so dusty that the house is full of dust though the windows and doors are kept shut, it comes in through every little crack and key hole'.* [41] These long cold winters and hot dry summers inevitably imposed a different rhythm on daily life in the town.

As most food was in poor supply in the winter apart from meat, the foreign families learnt to adopt Russian habits like preserving summer vegetables for use during the long winter months. Salted cabbage and dill pickles were stored in barrels, along with tomatoes and cucumbers and placed in underground pits called 'root cellars'. Cherries and plums from local orchards were also preserved or made into jam. Butter and potatoes were a luxury to be snapped up quickly if found in the market. Large blocks of ice were gathered in the winter to be stored in the cellars between layers of straw for use in the summer. In the winter, the deep snow largely confined people to their homes and great care was needed to avoid the occasional severe snowstorm. Annie Jones[42] who was tutor to the children of Arthur Hughes in the 1890s later recalled the result of one particularly heavy storm –

'We were on one afternoon on the point of going out for a sledge drive when we were persuaded not to go as the weather was threatening so we reluctantly stayed at home and it was very fortunate thing that we did for a severe snowstorm came on more like a whirlwind in nature. Early next morning 11 bodies were found frozen to death in the Steppes quite close to Hughesovka, including a boy whose mother hailed from Rhymney.'

But the cold weather also gave opportunities for fun; popular pastimes were skating and sledging with the traditional Russian 'troika' – a simple sledge drawn by three horses. Although extremely

---

41   Susan Edwards – ibid

42   Annie Gwen Jones – Recollections of Hughesovka (Colley Archive)

cold, it was dry and clear, not like the damp winter days in Britain and it was generally preferred to the stifling heat of summer. For a few brief weeks in spring a panoply of wild flowers burst forth across the steppes with violets, crocuses, forget-me-nots, buttercups, lilies of the valley and daffodils covering the ground. But all too soon, this display was gone and the steppes reverted to their barren, dreary norm. After the restrictions of winter, people welcomed the chance to escape the noise and dirt of Hughesovka on frequent summer picnics in the countryside and these seem fondly remembered. Because the edges of the town opened up straight onto the steppe, it was easy for families to enjoy nature on a warm summer's day. But nature in the Donbass could also be unpleasant or dangerous. In spring, there were regular plagues of rats and at various times through the year, the residents had to contend with invasions of flies, mosquitoes, cockroaches and even occasionally locusts. The steppe rat problem was so severe that the government instituted an extermination programme. All landowners and peasants were required to send the feet of rats they had killed to the local government offices as a form of tax. Failure to provide enough feet was met by a fine! The New Russia Company sent in thousands of feet each year. There were also wolves living on the open steppe and great care had to be taken when travelling, especially at night. With the cooler days of autumn, horse riding and hunting for foxes and hares were very popular with the men – the women were not normally allowed to participate due to the danger from wolves. The hunting parties were sometimes joined by officers from the local Cossack troop and with their excellent riding skills and fascinating tales of life in the Donbass they were a welcome addition to the group.

The first schools in Hughesovka were opened in the mid-1870s. There was a single-roomed school with just one teacher attended by some 80 local children and a school in the works for British children also with one teacher and 35 pupils initially. Parents had to pay fees at both schools – 50 kopeks per month for the local school and two roubles per month at the English school, though books were provided free of charge by the company. The fees were waived for children from poor families. These two schools were among the very first schools in the industrial settlements of the Donbass and even as late as 1885 there was only one other factory school in the whole Ekaterinoslav district. The children didn't start school until the age of seven and enjoyed three months of summer holidays. Wives and children could spend these long summer holidays at one of the Black Sea resorts. Most children of the longer-term British residents went initially to the town's English school and then were sent elsewhere in Russia or back to Britain for their secondary education. A few of the wealthier families employed foreign governesses. The local school was considerably expanded in 1890 with a building designed by the company's architect, Moldingauer and provided with well qualified teachers. In addition, the company was by then funding two other schools for Russians plus a church school, the private English school and two Jewish schools. The head teacher of the English school gave English lessons to some of the local factory workers and there was also a private tutor who apparently made a very handsome living from teaching English, French and German.

Many of the British children learnt to speak good Russian, becoming an important communication link with the locals and later, some even acted as interpreters for the company. Some ability in Russian and Ukrainian was also important for the British managers so as to communicate with the workforce. Indeed a few found that French or German was also beneficial given the mix of nationalities in Hughesovka. Initially, the local school head teacher was paid about the same as a skilled worker in the factory but as time went on and the staff increased, the pay ranking of teachers in the town rose so that they earned more than factory workers but this was still considerably less than the English school teachers. By the late 19th century, the annual cost to the company of the local school had risen to 10,000 roubles, considerably more per head than the amounts spent on health care or sanitation. By the time of the First World War, the company was supporting ten schools in and around the town which, with the other educational establishments, served over 5,600 pupils representing around 60% of school-age children, split evenly between boys and girls from all social classes. This was a remarkable achievement for a factory town and the amount and mix of children in education in Hughesovka was probably better than any other comparable settlement in the Donbass. Indeed, the number of 5,600 pupils in Hughesovka was approaching 25% of the total attending school in the whole Donbass region at this time.

The record on adult education was not as good as that for the children, despite the clear need due to poor literacy rates among the workers. Apart from the private tutoring mentioned earlier, there was little in the way of organised adult teaching programmes available until the 20th century, despite the fact that evening and Sunday classes had become popular in some of the larger Russian cities. However, things gradually took off in Hughesovka and classes were eventually offered in most traditional subjects, although take-up was very low with less than 400 attending classes in 1916. Part of the reason for this was undoubtedly the strenuous work for most employees leaving little energy for evening studies. But there was also the fact that adult education and teachers were closely linked with the various revolutionary movements, which made it some-what suspect as far as the authorities and company bosses were concerned. The same concerns by the authorities applied to public libraries (there were three in Hughesovka) but these proved to be more popular than adult classes and were used regularly. Around 1915 the company completed a new building housing a 2,000-seat auditorium with a stage and movie projection equipment plus a large library and reading room. A small charge was made to use these facilities and they proved very popular, especially the films.

Births and deaths were registered at the British Consulates in Odessa or Taganrog. Prior to the construction of the Protestant church, the

British families travelled to the Presbyterian church in Odessa to baptise their children. The British church of St George and St David, aptly named after the respective patron saints of England and Wales, had its own English minister and was visited once a year by the Bishop of Gibraltar in whose diocese the church lay. Throughout its history, the New Russia Company retained the right to appoint the chaplain. Church services took place daily at 10.00 and every Sunday at 8.30, 11.00 and 19.00, with a Sunday school at 8.30. The original chaplain's house was quite small but later he was provided with a spacious home with six living rooms, servants' quarters, and a carriage-house for the horse-drawn sleigh, with panoramic views over the steppe. There were also Orthodox and Catholic churches, a chapel, two synagogues plus a mosque and the company regularly contributed to their upkeep. The Orthodox church was built by public subscription in 1883 after the Russian workers had requested their own place of worship. The New Russia Company and Prince Lieven each donated 5,000 roubles and the workers contributed most of the remaining money needed by way of monthly deductions of 1% of their pay. Surprisingly, money was also raised for the church by the town's Jewish wine merchants, probably as a gesture to improve community relationships. The annual religious festivals were closely followed by both British and Russian families and relations between the Anglican and Orthodox churches were good. When the English chaplain Arthur Riddle died in 1911, the Orthodox priest conducted his funeral in the Anglican church. Shrovetide was a week-long celebration instead of a single day in Britain with lots of delicious pancakes. Easter was also a major event in the calendar with the giving of painted eggs, as in Britain and special Easter cakes, some two feet high! Suckling pigs were also traditional fare for the Russians at Easter time. The British brought with them their Christmas traditions with decorated trees and presents for the children and goose or turkey for Christmas Day dinner.

The British community tried to make their life in Russia as comfortable as possible and in many ways, thanks largely to Hughes' company, the facilities provided were as good as or better than they would have experienced at home. The range of cultural and social activities available in Hughesovka was certainly better than similar towns in the region. There were several sports and gymnastic clubs, tennis courts, football grounds plus a bicycle track. Croquet and golf (probably introduced by the Scottish residents) were also played regularly in the summer. An active social club arranged musical evenings and monthly dances as well as later showing films. The wife of one of the Hughes' sons (we don't know which) is listed in the programme for one of these concerts when she sang *'There is no home like my own'*. Hopefully this didn't make the British members of the audience too nostalgic! The Russians were generally very keen on all forms of music and singing. There was a works band and a string orchestra at the Russian school and in the summer, weekly concerts were held in the open air in the town centre. Indeed, one of Russia's most famous composers Sergei Prokofiev was born in a village near Hughesovka in 1890. The Hughes family were very active in the social life of the community as well as pursuing their own leisure interests. Weekly concert parties were held in Arthur Hughes' house and professional musicians were brought in occasionally. Once the company auditorium was built, amateur dramatics became popular and both English and Russian plays were performed. Travelling theatre groups also visited the town every summer as did a Russian circus. The Hughes family were keen on horses and hunting and even imported a pack of hounds from Merthyr Tydfil. Along with other company managers they rode, played sports, sailed, held fancy dress balls and in winter went sledging and skating.

Although Hughesovka was undoubtedly dirty and unhealthy, it was also relatively sophisticated when compared with similar sized towns in Russia. Henry Norman said of his visit to the Hughes family in Hughesovka,[43] *'As I entered the house, a Chopin waltz was being played on the piano. "You will find us in the billiard room after you have dressed," said my host. It seemed like a dream, so much civilisation ... after months*

43 Sir Henry Norman – ibid

spent in provincial Russia.' He went on to say it *'has no resemblance to a Russian provincial town; it is regularly laid out, its houses are solidly built and neatly kept, indeed many of them are luxurious'.* The level of culture among the local land-owning aristocracy was also generally high and they had a great love of music, reading and playing cards. However, despite their large estates and servants, few of them could be considered rich as most had mortgaged their lands years ago and they seemed disinclined to take up work to reduce their indebtedness. Although by the end of the 19th century a small Russian middle class was springing up, Hughesovka society as in most of provincial Russia was deeply divided between the well-born, educated minority and the mass of impoverished peasants and workers.

The risk of fire in Hughesovka was significant, especially in the hot dry summer months, with many wooden structures in the town as well as the dangers at the collieries and the steel works. So Hughes organised and trained a fire brigade, made up of a mixture of British and Russian workers, equipped with several horse-drawn pumps and hoses. A watch tower was also constructed by the company and manned by workers who had been injured. In 1913 the English school caught fire due to electric wiring problems but it was repaired and teaching soon resumed. A troop of 100 Cossack cavalry men was stationed near the town at Hughes' request to supplement Hughesovka's small police force and protect it from roaming bandits and robbers. The growing town was thought of as a wealthy place; there were several attacks on families in their homes and many of the foreign families employed a night watchman. The Cossacks provided a guard for the monthly transport of cash for the wages from Taganrog and their presence became even more vital during the riots in the 1890s. The company contributed to the cost of the Cossack troop as well as entirely funding Hughesovka's police force. By the end of the 19th century the latter had grown to three head constables plus around 80 men and was costing the company some 100,000 roubles a year. The telegraph and mail systems arrived with the railway link to the town and worked reasonably well. It took less than two weeks for a letter to arrive from Britain (not much slower than today's air mail) and the telephone was connected in the early 1900s. English newspapers were available in Hughesovka although these were subject to Russian censorship. They were all checked at the post office and if officials discovered any article thought to be critical of the government, it was either blotted out or the newspaper confiscated. Certain books deemed detrimental to the state were also banned by the government. The British also had to exercise caution about what they said and who they spoke to among the Russian community. The various revolutionary movements had supporters in both the works and the town generally and careless remarks could be misinterpreted. '*The police were watching and were looking into everything in great detail; and we had to be very careful.*' [44] The presence of revolutionary activists was noticed by a young soldier working on temporary assignment in Hughesovka inspecting shell cases for the army in 1916. He once came across seditious pamphlets placed in the ammunition packing boxes by workers at The New Russia Company proclaiming '*Workers of the world unite!*', presumably destined for soldiers at the front. He was also subsequently approached by some of the workers to join their group and help write their leaflets. [45]

Although the invention of the electrical telegraph is generally credited to the American Morse, the Russians claim that they were first. In 1833 P. L. Schilling, a Baltic inventor, constructed the world's first electromagnetic telegraph apparatus which pre-dates Samuel Morse's first working demonstration by several years. Certainly, by the time of Hughes' arrival in Ukraine, the Russian telegraph network was well established and there was a link to Britain via Norway and Scotland. Most large cities had the facility to transmit messages in English, French or German.

---

44 Annie Gwen Jones – ibid
45 Konstantin Paustovsky – Slow Approach of Thunder, 1965

By the end of the 19th century, the town centre boasted a fine parade of brick built shops and contemporary photos show a fine main street that could have been in Kiev or Moscow. There was also a co-operative store, a public garden, plus a local branch of the Russian Imperial Bank and by 1914, there were five banks in the town. In the 1897 census, there were more than 300 shops and stalls recorded plus five inns, ten wine cellars, four beer halls and one wholesale vodka store. However, the women were apparently frustrated at the lack of a good dress shop in the town and so made their own clothes or used local dressmakers. Many of the shops and stalls used pictures as signs to indicate the nature of their business due to the low literacy rate among the Russians.

The beer for the town was brewed by the South Russia Brewery, a separate limited company owned by the same shareholders as the New Russia Company. Drunkenness became a major problem both in the foreign community as well as the local population and British workers were occasionally sent home for 'misbehaviour' as it was euphemistically called. They seemed to learn to enjoy drinking vodka as much as the Russians. However, the comments about excessive drinking need to be balanced against what life was like in comparable British towns at the time. Merthyr Tydfil from where many of the original British workers came was well known at the time for its drunkenness and related high mortality rates. Hughes was no puritan, having met his future wife in the tavern next to the works in Newport but he knew the dangers of alcohol in a working environment and tried to ensure that Hughesovka's drinking places were not close to his works. As early as 1876 there was an argument between Hughes and Prince Lieven who had granted concessions for two new taverns near the factory gates. Hughes wrote to the government demanding they be closed immediately and demanding that no other taverns be opened near his works. This action by Prince Lieven and Hughes' lack of control over the situation was probably a factor in spurring him on to acquire all the land on which the town stood.

Some Donbass companies eventually took the drastic step of banning all taverns from their settlements but it was still relatively easy for a man to walk to the next town to drink. The problem in the Donbass was exacerbated by the high numbers of single workers, especially in the mines, who had no outside social influences to restrain their drinking habits. The Jews of the region came under regular criticism for being deeply involved in the sale of alcohol but they were not the only ones who were active in the trade in Hughesovka. As already noted, the company was effectively running its own brewery and the New Russia Company's chief bookkeeper, an Englishman called Church, also ran a tavern. The drink problem was one of the reasons cited by some Donbass companies for not paying their workers at fortnightly or monthly intervals. By withholding their pay for extended periods it was claimed that this helped reduce the frequency of drunkenness but this was probably not much more than an excuse as either the workers were usually able to obtain credit in the taverns, or, once paid, the drinking bouts lasted much longer. Although heavy drinking provided a temporary escape from the dangers of work and the dirt of their daily living conditions that many miners endured, it doesn't explain the habits of the factory workers who generally enjoyed a much better environment.

The economic and social cost of the excessive drinking was enormous both in Hughesovka and the Donbass generally. Not only were large sums of money wasted on drink that the workers could have better spent on improving their own lot or that of their family, but their health suffered, violence and social disorder ensued and after major drinking sessions, production from factories and mines was reduced. Attempts were made by the Congress of Mining Industrialists to curb the problem and the government was asked to impose its own monopoly on taverns and to regulate their opening hours, including closure on holidays and pay days. This provided some improvement but it was not until the start of the First World War when alcohol was banned entirely in Russia (apart from in first-class restaurants) that the situation changed markedly and as a result there was demand from company owners to extend this measure once the war was over. But as the USA found when it tried prohibition a little later, supply will always reach demand and soon bootleg operations in adjoining territories were supplying the deep-seated need for drink in the Donbass.

Hughesovka also had a regular Sunday bazaar and two annual fairs, one held after Easter and another in September. The weekly bazaars were very popular and well attended, not only by the residents of Hughesovka but also by thousands of peasants from the surrounding steppe. Hughes' town had become the epicentre of the region, industrially and culturally, and despite its shortcomings, Hughesovka sat in stark contrast to the surrounding poverty of the small villages and isolated mining settlements. Even though Hughesovka wasn't officially recognised as a town, it was becoming the de facto capital of the Donbass. A workers' co-operative was also established in 1888 in premises provided free of charge by the company and another by the company's workers at the Krivoi Rog mines in 1886. Although the Hughesovka co-operative ultimately grew to four stores, it unfortunately had a rather chequered history. One of its stores was looted and burned in the 1892 riots and it had to close in 1909 due to financial difficulties. It was later re-established, however, moving back into profit, and set up a library and book shop as well as offering loans to members to assist with the cost of education of their children. In its second phase the co-operative was almost exclusively run by company worker members and is a rare example of an independent institution operating for the benefit of local people. Also of interest is the fact that three photographic studios had been established by 1897 which partly explains the wealth of contemporary photographs available to us now as well as being a measure of the relative wealth of the town by then.

Yevgeny Khaldei, the renowned Red Army photographer, best known for his World War II photograph of a Russian soldier placing the Soviet Union's Red flag on top of the Reichstag building in Berlin in 1945, was born in Hughesovka in 1917. He was employed in the steelworks before taking up photography.

By 1901 the original town hospital had grown to 120 beds plus a staff of more than 60, including six doctors and a midwife. Additional hospitals were constructed at the mines outside the town. The company also operated a large 8,000-acre farm close to the town, producing fresh supplies for Hughesovka's inhabitants. In this and many other respects, Hughesovka was a forerunner of the company towns that were later to become so prevalent in Russia during the Soviet era. These towns grew up around a single local industry, dominating the town's entire economy, running farms, hospitals, schools plus all the social and recreational facilities.

Once the town had a rail link, travelling between England and Ukraine was tedious and long but relatively straightforward – at least when there wasn't a war, riots or revolution to contend with. The initial route out from Britain to Hughesovka was the same as that originally taken by Hughes and his workers when they first came. Although some continued to use this slower sea route, as the European rail network improved, the more normal route was by ferry from the port of Harwich across the English Channel to Ostend in Belgium and then on by train via Berlin, Warsaw, Kiev, Kharkov and finally on to Hughesovka; the whole journey taking around two weeks. Both routes gave the travellers the opportunity to visit interesting places and to shop for supplies on the way to Hughesovka or presents on the way home. The journey was not only undertaken at the start and end of the work contract but also to return home for holidays, to recover from illness or to escape turbulence in Russia. The numbers of British and foreign workers in Hughesovka varied over the years due to changes in the business cycle and patterns of investment in new technology at the works. The number of British workers probably never exceeded 150, which with families would have amounted to about 220 British people. A Russian survey in 1884 recorded 300 foreign nationals in Hughesovka and at its peak, in the 20th century, the foreign community in Hughesovka was a little over 700 people. However, not all of these came directly from their home country – some had come from elsewhere in Russia, where the men had been working at other iron works or building railways. In this context, the classification of foreigner excludes nationalities or ethnic groups that were part of the Russian Empire at the time such as Poles, Latvians or Belorussians. The population of Hughesovka was now increasing rapidly and by 1900 it had reached over 30,000 and in 1910 was 48,000. With an economic slowdown, instead of the earlier shortage of workers, the town was by now generating a labour surplus, like many others in western Russia. Some of the unemployed were 'encouraged' by the state to migrate to the east as colonists – Joubert[46] records meeting one such bedraggled group from Hughesovka at the railway station in Ekaterinoslav who were on their way to Manchuria. They seemed unsure of exactly where they were going and in Joubert's opinion were very ill equipped for the journey that lay ahead of them. Until the construction of the railway across Siberia, the colonists and many political exiles sent there had to walk. At least, the later travellers that went there by train could thank John Hughes for the small comfort of helping to provide the railway tracks. By the start of the First World War, Hughesovka's population had risen to over 50,000 and around 30% worked directly for the New Russia Company. In 1917 the population was 54,000, swollen by prisoners of war and other temporary workers brought in to expand production, with over 30 different nationalities. The Poles formed the largest foreign group followed surprisingly by the Greeks with Lithuanians, British, Latvians, Germans and Austrians making up the bulk of the

---

46   Carl Joubert – Russia As It Really Is

foreign population. This fascinating polyglot group also included a sprinkling of Persians, Czechs, Spanish, Italians, French, Belgians, Chinese, Swiss and Turks with at least one American family (during the 20th century one of the works managers was American as well as one of the hospital doctors).

All workers at the New Russia Company were entitled to housing and overall the quality of homes provided for both Russian and foreign workers was good. The award achieved by the company at the Nizhny Novgorod Exposition in 1896 was partly in recognition of the improvements it had made in workers' housing. A wide range of housing was built from apartments to rows of neat, white-washed, single-storey cottages and individual houses with gardens and stables. Photographs of the time show some of the foreigners' housing as being quite substantial buildings with well-tended gardens. When a new clergyman was needed for the British church in 1912, Archibald Balfour, a director of the New Russia Company, wrote to the Bishop of Gibraltar describing the accommodation available. '*The house intended for the chaplain contains 6 living rooms, kitchen, servants' and coachman's quarters, stable, carriage house, summer kitchen and ice cellar.*'[47] Depending on the individual worker's contract and position, accommodation was either free or subsidised and included heating and lighting. As we have seen, however, there were differences between the standards of accommodation provided for the miners and those in the works and it became impossible for the company to build enough accommodation to meet demand. Indeed, housing shortages and poor accommodation persisted well into the Soviet era as continued industrialisation swelled the urban population. Hughesovka did not have a dedicated drinking water supply until 1931, the first sewer system was only installed in 1933 and domestic gas was not available until 1934 within the city. There was overcrowding and conditions were sometimes sub-standard and unhealthy, leading to the spread of disease and several epidemics.

---

47   Susan Edwards – ibid

But Hughesovka's accommodation generally compared well with other provincial towns in Russia and even with similar industrial towns in Britain of the time. Without the official status of a town and the ability to raise local taxes, everything had to be funded by the New Russia Company. Given that by the 20th century there were many other commercial and manufacturing businesses in Hughesovka, plus the fact that the company employed only around 30% of the town's population, there were bound to be conflicts and different priorities.

As previously noted, many visitors to the town commented on the muddy streets, dirt and high levels of smoke and soot. As an industrial factory town this is not surprising but there were also adverse comments about certain aspects of Hughesovka's social life. One would expect in a town of miners and steel workers a certain amount of rough behaviour by the men but it seems that some of the women could be just as violent. Street fights between women were not uncommon and the men would bet on the outcome and often join in armed with *'leaded whips and knuckledusters ... then ... a Cossack patrol would trot up and scatter the crowd with their knouts'*.[48] Clearly there were stresses in the town's society brought about by an almost totally immigrant population of mixed nationalities and different religions plus the absence of any pre-existing social order that would otherwise have cushioned some of these tensions. As well as the natural differences between the various ethnic groups, part of the problem lay in the differences in pay and housing conditions between the miners and factory workers. With some justification, the miners continually felt that they were not treated as well as the factory workers and this was one of the root causes of social unrest and the periodic strikes that occurred in Hughesovka. The factory workers looked down on the miners and there was only limited social exchange between the two groups of workers. There were also concerns among the residents about the level of

---

48   Konstantin Paustovsky – ibid

crime and the activities of various criminal gangs in and around the town. The Donbass was seen as a frontier area and its rapid development had attracted a number of former convicts, criminals, political fugitives and vagrants by the turn of the century. As the principal town in the area and the richest, Hughesovka inevitably drew in more than its fair share of these people and the local police force struggled at times to cope.

Whether Hughes (and later his sons) had any specific model in mind when building and developing Hughesovka is unknown. Its relatively haphazard expansion in the early years suggests there was no specific plan at first. However, the later growth of the town with a much more formal layout and the hiring of a company architect indicate that Hughes and his sons recognised the need for planning. Whether he was aware of the trend among some Victorian industrialists in Britain to build model company villages and towns for their workers is unknown but there are some interesting similarities. At the time of Hughes' arrival in Ukraine, the most famous was Saltaire in West Yorkshire, established in 1853 by Sir Titus Salt, a leading industrialist in the Yorkshire woollen industry. The name of the village is a combination of the names of the founder and that of the adjacent river. Salt moved his entire business (five separate mills) from Bradford to this site and constructed a complete new village to house his workers. He built neat stone houses for his workers, a vast improvement on their previous slums in Bradford, complete with wash-houses with running water, bath-houses, a hospital, as well as an Institute for recreation and education, with a library, a reading room, a concert hall, billiard room, science laboratory and gymnasium. There was also special housing for the poor plus allotments, a park and a boathouse. A later model town was Port Sunlight near Birkenhead in North West England, founded in 1888 by the Lever family. Since its development was well publicised in Britain at the time, it may have provided some inspiration for the Hughes family and again there are some common themes with Hughesovka. By 1909 Port Sunlight had a theatre and concert hall, library, gymnasium, open-air swimming men's club and various societies and self-improvement activities for those interested in literature, music and art. Although the Lever experiment was not without its critics, some of whom saw the family as benevolent despots, controlling the lives of their workers, contemporary studies revealed high standards of health, morality and a strong sense of community. The quality and quantity of output also demonstrated the success of the new town.

With the British influence, football became very popular in Hughesovka and there were matches between British and Russian teams. In the early 20th century the town had one of Russia's leading football teams. In the summer of 1913 it competed against teams from 12 other cities for the very first Russian inter-city cup in Odessa. The cup was actually won by Odessa, beating St Petersburg 4-2 in the final. The teams involved were from across Russia including Moscow, Rostov, Kharkov, Kiev, Sebastopol and Hughesovka. David James, one of the New Russia Company's British workers played for the team – it was his last game before joining the British army in 1914.

CHAPTER EIGHT
John Hughes and His Family

Inevitably when considering Hughes' achievements, a range of questions come to mind. What kind of man was he? What lay behind his decision to go to Russia? What were the driving forces behind his business philosophy and approach? It is hard to understand exactly what motivated John Hughes to go to live in Ukraine, leaving his family behind and to take on the considerable risks and responsibilities of setting up a new venture in the remote Donbass region. He was a family man of 55, enjoying a successful career as a company director in London, the hub of the vast British Empire, with all the stimulus and excitement associated with the heyday of the Victorian era. Although not wealthy, he was financially very secure and led a comfortable life. But despite these achievements, perhaps he was not totally at ease with his situation and position in the society around him. Although he had done well and knew many famous people, he was still a self-made man with little education and of relatively humble origins in an age and society where class and family background meant so much. It may have been difficult for Hughes and especially his wife Elizabeth to feel at ease in the social milieu in which they now found themselves. As was often the case in these situations in Victorian Britain, it was the next generation that was more easily able to move up the social ladder

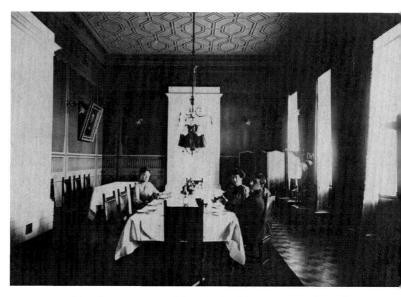

The dining room of the Hughes' home c.1900 *(GRO)*

The sitting room of the Hughes' home c.1900 *(GRO)*

The Hughes' home viewed from the Steppe

The Hughes' family country dacha *(GRO)*

The Hughes' family home in Hughesovka c.1900 *(GRO)*

The Hughes' home and garden *(GRO)*

A Hughes family summer picnic *(GRO)*

Hughes family household staff *(GRO)*

John Hughes (centre back) with family and friends (Ivor, Arthur and John James are bottom right) *(GRO)*

The Hughes family and friends on horseback 1892 *(GRO)*

Right: John James
Hughes (seated)
and Ivor Hughes

Far right: Arthur
Hughes with his
two daughters and
their tutor, Annie
Gwen Jones
(GRO)

and three of Hughes' sons as well as his daughter all married advantageously. Elizabeth was probably less ambitious than her husband and content with raising their children and day-to-day family life in their Greenwich home. We know very little of Hughes' personal life and circumstances in London at this time. But after 25 years of marriage it is possible his drive and ambition led him to look for some new stimulation. Although Hughes had successfully built up the business in Millwall, the future of the area's shipbuilding and iron working industries was looking less secure as other regions in Britain became more competitive. The areas around the Tyne and Wear in the North of England and Glasgow in Scotland were fast emerging as the new centres of heavy industry. Perhaps there was simply not the right new opportunity or enough space for the successful businessman in Britain. At the time of the visit by Guern and Todleben, Hughes may already have been considering a career change. Unsettled at home, the opportunity to move overseas, forming a new company and combining all his talents and experience to exploit the vast Ukrainian coal and iron deposits may have seemed exactly the right offer at the right time. But it would be no easy task as Hughes' main experience at Uskside and Millwall was in marine engineering and the manufacture of iron plates. He was to now concentrate on coal mining and smelting iron for rail production and his success in making this transition in a foreign environment is a measure of the abilities of the man.

The general situation in Russia in the latter half of the 19th century was not one that encouraged entrepreneurial activity. Few of the businessmen or industrialists who did exist, whether Russian or foreign, could be viewed as dynamic. In the Ukraine, the region's riches were only being slowly exploited by a few Russian and foreign businessmen and so remained largely untouched. Many were small-scale operators, especially in coal mining, and they often invested only for a few years before moving on. Most preferred to live in Moscow, Kharkov or Taganrog leaving day-to-day operations in charge of a hired manager. Hughes and his sons were to be one of the rare exceptions. Their commitment, energy and interest in developing the New Russia Company would provide an enduring legacy for the enterprise and Hughesovka as well as the region overall. They effectively introduced the Industrial Revolution to this part of Russia and made a substantial contribution to the growth of industrial capitalism and the modernisation of Russia.

The ultimate success of Hughes and his company was driven by a combination of three principal factors – a determination to make good profits for his shareholders, his expertise in the application of modern technology and processes plus a deep-seated concern for the community under his care. Hughes unquestionably delivered good profits for his shareholders who of course included himself but this was no easy or automatic result. Others, including Prince Kochubei, had failed to seize the opportunity available and not all foreign businessmen that followed Hughes to the Donbass made good profits. As in so many things Hughes was the exception rather than the rule. But it took many years before any dividends were paid as Hughes first made sure the company had generated sufficient cash reserves to continue to grow and develop. For him the basic rule was that the prospect of business comes first, the profit comes second. His caution in this respect typifies one of his traits of character; he rarely seems to have made quick decisions in running the company, preferring to carefully consider and evaluate his options. But once he took a decision, he showed exemplary determination to see it through and rarely changed or modified his chosen course of action. There is no doubt that Hughes proved very adept at introducing and utilising modern technology and although the changeover to steel proved a major challenge, he successfully overcame it.

Existing photographs of Hughes show a round-faced, bearded, broad-shouldered man with a kind, considerate face. He could have been a school teacher or church minister and there is ample evidence to show he was a caring and considerate person. He was

154

a man of spirit and certainly never afraid of hard work. Those who knew Hughes well describe him as being exceptionally good humoured, kindly but also very shrewd. Benevolent though he was, Hughes was certainly also stern, patriarchal and authoritarian in the way that he managed the company and the town and at times could be brusque in his dealings with people. But despite this he evidently inspired great loyalty and admiration among his employees and others with whom he dealt outside the company. The fact that many of his key managers such as John John, Alexander Cameron, Percy Cartwright and Charles Perry stayed with him for many years through thick and thin illustrates this. Another point of reference is the Russian engineer Nicholai Lebedev who was sent by the government to Hughesovka to watch over Hughes' performance on his contract. From his initial very negative reports rubbishing the company's products, his tone gradually changed to the extent that he became a firm supporter of Hughes and his methods. When Hughes died in 1889, Lebedev wrote an obituary full of praise, describing him as *one of the most energetic and honourable persons engaged in the mining industry*. [49]

Hughes and his family retained complete control of both the New Russia Company and Hughesovka until 1917, running it as virtually their own private estate (although still ultimately responsible to the Russian government and company shareholders). Hughes no doubt valued the freedom and independence his position gave him; he was the technical expert as well as the driving force in the enterprise. Later, as his reputation in the industry and with government grew, he also gained a status that he could not have achieved had he stayed in London. The power and lifestyle of the Hughes family was comparable in some ways to that of the 19th century Russian aristocracy with their control over vast tracts of land and thousands of peasants and their families. Indeed, the way in which the town and factory were referred to in Russian as 'Hughes' town'

49 Theodore Friedgut – ibid

and 'Hughes' factory' echoed the Russian aristocracy's system of giving their family name to their estates. Hughes was like a local Tsar, ultimately controlling virtually every aspect of economic and social life in his town. A comparison can also be made with the wealthy English ironmasters of Merthyr and Dowlais who lived in grand homes overlooking their works. But Hughes was no aristocrat and although the family home in Hughesovka was substantial, it needed to be to accommodate close to 20 people plus servants. Although the family also benefited from a large two-storey dacha outside the town, their main house was close to the works and not a mock castle on a hill like the homes the Crawshay and Guest families built. However, Hughes never forgot his early days in Wales and he may well have had thoughts about the New Russia Company becoming a dynastical enterprise like Cyfarthfa, being passed down from one generation to another. By the 1880s he knew that he had built a business and town that would last beyond his death and the presence of four of his sons in Hughesovka as managers in the company indicates this was a possibility. At the very least, there must surely have been a gleam in Hughes' eyes when his company overtook Cyfarthfa in terms of production and number of employees. Some of Hughes' general approach to running his business may also have originated from his early years working at Cyfarthfa as there were several marked similarities between the operation of the New Russia Company and that of the Crawshays. Both regulated the lives of their workforce in the factory as well as attempting to control them at home with a view to providing a framework in which they could better themselves. The idea of self-improvement was an important belief amongst Victorian industrialists, largely inspired by the writings of Samuel Smiles (1812-1904), whose massive bestseller 'Self-help' was published in 1859. His basic concepts were that 'heaven helps those who help themselves' and for society to progress, individuals have to make the most of their lives, proving their moral worth by working hard and doing good. Hughes must have been familiar with such a well known book and he certainly seems to have subscribed to the view that society will get better if individuals concentrate on making themselves prosperous and even men of humble origin can achieve great things if they avoid immorality and work hard to improve themselves. As Smiles wrote, *'The spirit of self-help is the root of all genuine growth in the individual.'*

The technology of the New Russia Company together with Hughes' Victorian capitalist values and paternalistic management style would have been very unfamiliar to the peasant workers arriving in Hughesovka from all over Russia. However, there would have been a general understanding and acceptance of the day-to-day control over their lives to ensure the factories, mines and town all worked successfully. The peasants were used to the rigid boundaries of their home villages as Russian society at the time was strictly regulated from central government downwards and therefore Hughes' overall approach was also accepted by the Tsarist authorities who were suspicious of any individual freedoms. Over the years, Hughes and his sons were regularly visited by a variety of Russian and foreign businessmen, officials and bankers keen to know more about his methods and approach to running the company and town. Understandably, they were not always forthcoming in their responses to requests for information and they generally remained tight-lipped about details of their business. On occasions it seems they would exaggerate or tell outlandish stories about the problems faced by the company and its achievements. This secrecy on the part of Hughes and his family led to some confusion and misunderstanding about what had really been achieved in Hughesovka and as a result the company was criticised in some contemporary reports. Paul Chapuy, a graduate from the Ecole des Mines in Paris visited Hughes in 1887 as part of a study tour analysing various companies in Russia. He commented in his thesis that Hughes was rather rude and refused to furnish any precise information. A Russian visitor complained *'we had to visit the factory without any guide and were given no quantitative information'.*[50] Even

---

50 Theodore Friedgut – ibid

the Credit Suisse bankers who visited the company annually often came away with misinformation and failed to get to the bottom of how the business operated. As well as seeking technical and financial information about his coal and steel operations, visitors were keen to explore how he managed and retained his workforce. They were particularly interested in the company's investments in social assets like housing and schools. As pointed out above, these costs were proving to be an important and necessary cost of doing business in Ukraine. Many of the foreign industrialists were finding out that they had seriously under-estimated this overhead in their original project budgets and were later forced to seek additional capital. The canny Hughes probably felt that in a competitive market, providing such information was not in his company's best interests! It is worth noting that with one exception, the other steel companies that followed Hughes into the Donbass region did not locate directly on the coal deposits. Their concerns about the availability of local labour led them to set up and expand near existing towns.

In Soviet times, Hughes was labelled as a capitalist exploiter of labour, solely interested in profits who failed to look after his workers and 'ruled' over a polluted, unsanitary company town with few amenities and poor governance. These criticisms are a distortion of the truth and clearly unfair. There is abundant evidence that Hughes was genuinely interested in his workers and cared for those around him and didn't always take the decisions that could have maximised company profitability. If financial gain were his sole motivation, he would have relocated to St Petersburg much earlier to enjoy his wealth. Hughes and his company led the field in south Russia in the 19th century in housing the workers and their families plus the rest of the town's population as well as providing other social amenities and benefits. No Russian entrepreneurs came forward to build houses for rent to the workers in Hughesovka. Neither the state nor local government stepped in to fund the schools or hospitals and religious bodies were no better, leaving the construction of churches and synagogues to the company. Wages at the New Russia Company were significantly higher than at similar companies elsewhere in Russia and the terms and conditions of employment were also generally more favourable. Although rightly criticised for not doing enough for his miners, the overall situation in Hughesovka's mines was considerably better than in comparable mining companies in the Donbass or other parts of Russia. If this were not the case, Hughes would not have been able to successfully attract and retain new workers while other foreign companies were complaining of shortages. Hughesovka was a town that grew out of and still depended on coal mining and steel and therefore would never be a garden city. In the 20th century it may not have been as relatively advanced as it was earlier but it was successful and provided jobs and homes for thousands of workers and established the industrial base for the city of Donetsk as it is today. Indeed it could be argued that the company town formula established by Hughes and subsequent foreign industrialists in south Russia became the norm for the whole of Russia in Soviet times. He would have considered himself to be firm but fair in his dealings with his workers and was not afraid to roll up his sleeves and lead by example. Indeed in the very early days he could be found working from dawn to dusk stripped to the waist helping to build the works, much to the confusion of the Russians who were unsure whether he was a worker or the manager.

The special provisions he made for the poor and disadvantaged show his humane side and his policies were carried on by his sons. Hughes' kindness and thoughtfulness were commented on both in contemporary documents and by several of his employees in their subsequent memories of life in Hughesovka. He was evidently well liked and respected by his employees and must also have had good relationships with his sons who not only came to join him in Russia but stayed on after his death to run the company. Hughes was clearly a skilful negotiator as he proved when finalising his original agreement with the Russian government and later when negotiating the purchase of land or mining rights. While not afraid to speak his mind, almost to the point of bluntness, he was also a diplomat in the sense that he knew how to make the right connections and influence people. This was evident from his time in London and was repeated in his contacts with the Russians in St Petersburg where in due course, Hughes became accepted into the highest governmental circles, acquiring many supporters for his bold plans. The Russian Admiralty considered Hughes to be hard working and energetic and the Tsar presented him with a diamond ring in recognition of his services to Russia. Hughes not only lobbied the government on behalf of his company and industrial sector but also on wider issues of trade and finance. Both Hughes and later his sons were also well known amongst the British community in St Petersburg and mixed with many of the established merchant and business families there. One of the fascinating things about Hughes is that he achieved so much despite his limited education. John Baddeley who in the 1880s was the St Petersburg correspondent for The London Standard and author of several books about Russia, became good friends with Hughes and he later wrote of him that '*to the day of his death he could not write; and could only read print with difficulty, script not at all*'. [51] It is hard to verify the accuracy of this statement but as Baddeley knew Hughes well and was impressed by him, it is unlikely he would lie or exaggerate. If it was correct, it makes Hughes' achievements all the more remarkable, running what was at the time one of the world's largest companies as well as a sizeable town, all in a foreign country. It also helps explain the total absence of any surviving personal correspondence by Hughes in any of the archives. The official letters and documents that do exist were presumably dictated by Hughes to an assistant. Hughes' limited ability in reading and writing must have been a source of great frustration to him and it is strange that a man with so many talents never learnt these skills in later life. However, it obviously didn't hold him back in his

---

51   John Baddeley – ibid

career and as his friend Baddeley acknowledged, this shortcoming was counterbalanced by his ability to read men, understand them and to rule them.

Although Hughes was an intensely practical man with minimal education or book learning, he took great interest in the history of iron working, sword smiths and related mythology. During occasional meetings with John Baddeley in the Hotel Angleterre in St Petersburg, he loved to exchange stories about the Cimmerians, Chalybes and in particular the Celtic races which he believed were the world's best blacksmiths. Hughes held the theory that the development and advance of early civilisations was closely matched to their capability as blacksmiths and the manufacture of high quality swords.

The Chalybes were an ancient tribe that settled in north Anatolia, near the shores of the Black Sea and are thought to be the ancestors of the Georgians. They are credited with the invention of iron working and Χάλυψ, the tribe's name in Greek, means tempered iron or steel, a term that passed into Latin as *chalybs*, "steel" which in turn, is possibly the origin for *Excalibur*, the name of King Arthur's legendary sword. The Cimmerians were also an ancient tribe that settled in south Ukraine around 2000BC.

Looking back almost 200 years after his birth, John Hughes remains something of an enigma. It is frustrating that we know so little about the real man, his daily life and inner thoughts or feelings. But it is clear he was a courageous visionary who recognized the potential of southern Ukraine as his 'niche' and successfully managed to make his plans come true, primarily owing to his engineering talents, management skills and determination. He was a good planner and organiser, able to handle considerable detail without losing track of the big picture. His knowledge and skills allowed him to successfully manage coal and iron mines, complex metallurgical factories, railway construction, company finances and marketing as well as having time to organise housing, hospitals, schools and a company farm. He was what would be called today a multi-tasker, active in all aspects of the business. Like his more famous contemporary Andrew Carnegie who emigrated from Britain to the USA and developed the Pittsburgh steel industry, John Hughes belongs to that special group of entrepreneurs who know the value of profits but who are also able to invent and successfully apply their know-how in a socially just manner. He had the energy, commitment and devotion to the task of building a modern industrial enterprise plus a thriving town to support its activities.

When Hughes moved to Russia, he left behind in Greenwich his wife Elizabeth, his eldest child Sarah, then aged 24, and his five sons, John James Hughes aged 22, Arthur aged 18, Ivor aged 15, Albert aged 12 and Owen aged 11. We know little of the early life of Hughes' children and their schooling in London, apart from Albert. He pursued a technical education and took a job in a chemical laboratory in London, studying physics, chemistry and mineralogy at night school at King's College.[52] This proved to be an excellent preparation for his later position in the New Russia Company in charge of the blast furnaces and analytical laboratories. Sadly, his youngest son Owen died in 1880, still in his early twenties – the same year that his wife Elizabeth also died and this must have been a very tragic year for Hughes. The precise dates when each of Hughes' four sons joined him in Hughesovka also remain unknown, though given the spread in their ages they presumably arrived at different times. Their decision to join their father in Russia shows they must have been close to him and held him in good regard. The involvement of Hughes' sons in managing

---

52   Theodore Friedgut – ibid

the company would have required the support of the board so there must have been confidence in their individual capabilities.

As the eldest son, John James Hughes probably arrived first in Hughesovka. For all of his time there he was single and although a hard worker, he no doubt enjoyed the life of a well-to-do young bachelor. After the death of his father, John James became managing director of the New Russia Company and based himself in St Petersburg periodically visiting Hughesovka. In the 1890s he eventually married a Jewish woman, Alice Hirschfield from London, some 25 years younger than himself although she continued to live in London where John James would periodically visit her. Despite this disjointed matrimonial arrangement, they had two daughters and a son and John James moved permanently to London in 1905 but remained very much involved with the company until his death in 1917.

Arthur David Hughes supervised the steel works at Hughesovka and took over as resident director, a role he shared with his brother Ivor. He married a woman from Wales called Augusta James and they lived together in Hughesovka and had five children, all born in the town. He was the only one of the five surviving children that married to follow his roots and wed someone from Wales. Like John James, he also died in 1917.

Ivor Hughes spent the shortest period in Hughesovka of the four brothers. He returned to England in 1905 and married a Wilhelmina de Hart. They had two daughters and a son and lived in Sussex where he kept racehorses until his death in 1916. The Hughes family had been keen on breeding and racing horses in Hughesovka so this was a continuation of family interests in Russia.

Albert Llewellyn Hughes was the youngest of the four surviving sons. After his father's death in 1889, Albert became a department manager responsible for the blast furnaces and analytical laboratories at Hughesovka. Albert suffered badly from tuberculosis and was sent to Italy for the winter. During his time there he met and fell in love with a married woman, Katherine Fischer. He managed to arrange a deal with her husband, paying him a large sum of money to divorce Katherine. They married in St Petersburg and then settled in Hughesovka with Katherine's young daughter from her previous marriage. The latter unfortunately died soon after their arrival but they subsequently had two daughters of their own. Katherine became infamous in the town as the woman Hughes had bought. On Albert's death in 1907, she moved to St Petersburg and married into the Tolstoy family and both daughters subsequently married Russian noblemen. Sadly, the family had an extremely difficult time with the Bolsheviks in 1918 and the husband of one of the daughters was buried alive. The surviving members of the family fled the country and all ended up in France.

John Hughes died in June 1889 in St Petersburg at his favourite hotel, the Hotel Angleterre, aged 74. He had been running the New Russia Company for 20 years as managing director and was still active until his death. He was on business in St Petersburg and collapsed while out for a walk in the centre. He left an estate valued at over £90,550 (over £9m today). In his will Hughes bequeathed the majority of his estate to his four sons. In addition, he left his eldest son, John James, the diamond ring given to him by the Tsar plus the silver tea and coffee service silver salver presented to Hughes by the workmen at Millwall. Hughes wanted these items to be passed on in the family as heirlooms. He also gave 40 ordinary shares in the New Russia Company to both John James and Albert in recognition of *their unsparing exertions and the support they have given me …. during many anxious years*. Hughes was buried in the Norwood cemetery in London, alongside his wife and youngest son Owen, both of whom had died in 1880. His three surviving sons, Albert, Ivor and John James, were also ultimately buried in the family grave in Norwood. His daughter Sarah, who had married and continued to live in London, survived until 1929.

But Hughes' death was neither the end of the company nor the town he had built. The running of the company now fell to his four sons who had all been involved with the business for some years. Hughes had taken care to train each of his sons in different aspects of managing the company and it was clearly his intention that the New Russia Company should remain a family-run affair after his death. John James Hughes took over as managing director, based like his father in St Petersburg. Arthur and Ivor became directors and shared the day-to-day running of the company in Hughesovka. Albert was responsible for the blast furnaces and laboratories. With a recovery in the Russian market in the 1890s, the Hughes sons expanded the business considerably, rebuilding the existing four furnaces and adding two new ones. Production of iron was tripled, making the New Russia Company the largest in Russia. But in the early 1900s, production fell as the economy slowed again, with further disruptions caused by the war with Japan in 1904-05 and the 1905 revolution, although these same problems affected other companies in Russia.

In 1905 Arthur, Ivor and Albert and their families all moved to St Petersburg, joining their brother John James. They left John Anderson in charge of the works and Archibald Balfour who had been made a director of the company in 1901 took over as commercial director. Balfour continued in this role in Hughesovka until 1912 when he returned to Britain, remaining a director of the company until his death. The Balfour family had been active partners of Hughes since the beginning of the enterprise. Balfour's son Montague also came to live in Hughesovka and became involved in running the New Russia Company's farm, having earlier studied agriculture in Canada. The fact that one of the railway stations near the works was called Balforovo is an indication of the important involvement of the Balfour family in the company and town. Balfour's daughter Edith was born in St Petersburg and became a famous novelist and left-wing activist. She married Alfred Lyttleton a British politician and famous sportsman and she was a close friend of Arthur Balfour (no relation), British prime minister from 1902 to 1905. John Anderson was English but born in Russia and had extensive experience of industry in the Donbass region. His daughter was born in the Hughesovka and the family remained in the Donbass through the civil war into the early 1920s. Anderson was subsequently replaced by the company's first Russian works manager Adam Svitsyn who subsequently had the unenviable task of managing the business through the 1917 revolution. Rees Richards and an American, Revillon, were the two chief assistants to Svitsyn in 1914. Whether this is the Albert Revillon recorded as a director of the company in 1906 or one of his relatives is not clear.

Adam Svitsyn left the New Russia Company when the Bolsheviks took over but remained in the steel industry becoming a well known metallurgist in Stalin's time and was technical director of the Southern Steel Company. His career came to an abrupt end in 1928 when in one of Stalin's early purges he was removed by order of the Politburo, arrested by the GPU and accused of misuse of state funds. His subsequent fate is not known.

Although steel rails and iron bars continued to form the bulk of the company's output, its range of products was expanded in 1909 to include large steel sections for bridges, up to 180 metres long. The increase in production during the First World War gave a boost to company sales and profits and there was renewed confidence and investment in both the business and the town. At the 46th annual meeting of the company held in 1914, the chairman, Archibald Balfour, informed the shareholders that *the deposit of ore which they possessed was, so far as indication went, illimitable. The existence of this great source of supply gives every hope for the future success of the Company, in view of the fact that the coal and limestone deposits they possess are among the richest beds hitherto discovered in the Russian Empire*.[53] In 1916, the company hired a well known Swedish architect, Nils Settergren, to lead a new design project but sadly, he died of cholera in 1917 before his work was finished. The 1916 company accounts showed assets of £3.69 million and a handsome dividend of £120,000 was paid to shareholders. John James, who was still a director of the New Russia Company, died in June 1917 aged 59. He was the last of the Hughes to be involved with the company and his death marked the end of almost 50 years of family involvement.

Under a new board of directors, production continued, despite increasing problems and material shortages during the turmoil of the Bolshevik Revolution. In 1919 the Bolsheviks seized the company and took control of the town and all the company's assets in Russia. It was perhaps fortuitous that none of the sons remained when the business started by their father was abruptly seized by the Bolsheviks. However, this was not quite the end of the New Russia Company; the board of directors remained in place and the shareholders continued to support the company. Under local management, the company carried on and even took out a series of loans in 1918, 1919 and 1920 for extensions to the works. In the company's annual report for 1920, its net assets had grown further and were shown to be over £4 million (over £133m today). But after the Bolshevik takeover of the company in 1919, the writing was on the wall for the shareholders. No more dividends were paid and the subsequent refusal of the new Russian government to provide any compensation meant that the shares were now worthless. The New Russia Company was finally dissolved on June 12th 1970 – almost exactly 100 years after John Hughes arrived in Ukraine to found the business. In 1924, the Communists renamed Hughesovka and it was called Stalino until 1961 when it took on its current name of Donetsk. Hughes would surely have found some irony in the renaming of his town after the then leader of the Soviet Union.

---

53 George Hume – ibid

In replacing the name of Hughes with that of Stalin, the most important man in the country, the Soviets effectively gave implicit recognition to the importance of Hughesovka.

CHAPTER NINE
Later Years

By the mid 1890s, the coal and steel industry in south Russia had become well established and a vital part of the country's economy. It was now one of the world's most technologically advanced industrial centres, yet unlike comparable complexes in Europe or the USA, it sat in a poor and under-developed market. Large state orders were inadequate to fill the growing domestic manufacturing capacity. To try to fill their factories, most steel rail makers had diversified into other metal products – both for industrial and household use – some even established their own retail outlets. But low household incomes and a continuing propensity among the wealthier classes and regional administrations for imported products meant sales remained low. The New Russia Company, however, did not follow this route due to its success in obtaining a high level of government contracts and continued to concentrate on its core products.

Given the state's regulatory role, its control of tariffs and subsidies plus its influence over prices and officials, the industry felt the need to try to engage with state bodies and lobby them. The Congress of Mining Industrialists to which the New Russia Company belonged had existed for some time but it was felt that a more powerful body was needed. Accordingly, the first step was the formation of the

Association of Southern Coal and Steel Producers, which became a very well organised industry pressure group in the period leading up to 1914. It also set up a Society for Aid to Families of Miners as well as its own technical college – the Ekaterinoslav Higher Mining School. This association was later followed by the Society for the Sale of Products of the Metallurgical Industry – better known as Prodamet. Despite a steady stream of detailed policy recommendations aimed at developing a more integrated economic policy and wider allocation of state orders, Prodamet's results were limited. This was partly because several large companies including the New Russia Company did not join this new organisation and counter lobbying by northern industrialists (who had different objectives) supported by the St Petersburg government bureaucracy who feared loss of power and influence.

The reasons why the New Russia Company largely stayed outside this association are not fully clear. However, its dependence on state orders was great and a wider share-out of this business among all members would have severely impacted it financially. Hughes had been careful to build up good relationships in government circles over the years and the company preferred to rely on these rather than the cartel. In addition, it is likely that joining a cartel ran against the Victorian principles of free trade and independence that Hughes and the New Russia Company stood for. At one acrimonious meeting of the Congress of Mining Industrialists, Arthur Hughes reportedly said that the industry's problems were the result of too many inefficient firms and he would be happy to help the industry by bankrupting some of his competitors. Much of the discussions in the association were taken up with labour supply and related social issues but since Hughes' company was not experiencing any labour shortages and its social programmes were already in advance of his competitors, there were less likely benefits in participating. Also by the 20th century, the cartel appeared to increasingly have broader political objectives which would not have fitted in with the New Russia Company's position.

In 1908 the south Russia cartel moved to strengthen its situation in the face of a sharp reduction in government rail orders. A new organisation was formed known as the Company of Metallurgical Factories, Mines and Pits, replacing Prodamet. It successfully grouped over 80% of the region's iron producers as well as other manufacturers elsewhere in the country. But again, many of its objectives remained unfulfilled in the face of regional rivalries and government intractability towards any industrial combination that might become too powerful and develop into a political threat. The government did accept the value of supporting a vibrant industrial economy with state orders, tariff protection, grant loans and an improved banking system but did not want to lose any control or risk price rises as a result of price fixing by a cartel. Whilst accepting the existence of these industry bodies, the government kept them under close surveillance and officials always attended or even chaired their meetings.

It is clear that both Hughes and later his sons gave serious thought to selling the New Russia Company on several occasions. Given the very real problems in running the business in a foreign country, dealing with the various ups and downs of the Russian economy, the harsh climate, increasing competition and in Hughes' case, advancing age, it is not a surprise. The first documented mention of such action shows this was a possibility as early as 1885. Paul Chapuy, who we met in chapter six, stated following a visit with Hughes in 1887 that Hughes told him he *'had almost closed for good in 1885'*. Although Chapuy does not give any reasons, we can conclude that this was probably a result of a combination of factors. In many ways, it would have been a good time for Hughes and his fellow shareholders to get out. The company had grown well, making good profits, and held a valuable position in the Russian market with a strong reputation. However, the rise in the number of new enterprises and the downturn of the early 1880s had resulted in excess capacity and meant hard times for the Russian iron and steel sector, including the New Russia

171

Company. Also, to maintain a leading position in the market place, significant new investment would be required. In addition, Hughes was by now 70 years old and potential retirement would have appeared attractive. We do not know why nothing happened at this time. It may have been due to Hughes' dogged determination to carry on (perhaps for the sake of his sons) but most likely it was as a result of the imposition by the state of a new tariff on imported cast iron which improved the relative position of domestic producers like Hughes. In 1887 the government also renewed its tariff on pig iron for a further ten years, which was an additional benefit to the New Russia Company. It could now sell pig iron to St Petersburg and Moscow for some 20% less than imported products. By the end of 1913, Hughes' three surviving sons (John James, Arthur and Ivor) were clearly looking again at the possibility of a sale. John James and Arthur had by then relocated from Hughesovka to St Petersburg and were no longer involved in the day-to-day running of the company and Ivor had returned to England. In December 1913, they held discussions regarding a possible sale with a Frenchman Jules Goujon, based in Moscow. He was well established in the Russian metallurgical industry and obtained a three-month option with Dreyfus & Company to buy the New Russia Company. But he was unable to find suitable finance to proceed with the purchase and his option lapsed. Although the company's shareholders could not know it at the time, this was to be their last chance to achieve a sale. The outbreak of war in 1914 and the ensuing revolution in Russia meant that the shareholders had no option but to ride out the storm and hope for a peace and stability that never came.

In the hundred years or so before Hughes and his group of British workers arrived in Hughesovka, a fascinating variety of men from Britain had come to work and settle in Russia, primarily in the St Petersburg area. The initial contacts between Britain and Russia that flowed from the founding of the original Russian company (see page 33) really gathered pace with Peter the Great in the 18th century. He brought British sailors, engineers, mathematicians, merchants and doctors to the new Russian capital, some of whom stayed for many years making important contributions to the life of the city. Peter trusted British specialists and was impressed with their capabilities, appointing them to some of the highest posts in the government. St Petersburg's first governor Roman Bruce was descended from the Scottish royal family and his brother was a field marshal in the Russian army. The shipbuilder Richard Brown was in charge of building Russia's first Baltic Fleet. The first British Ambassador to Russia was appointed in 1716 and the growth in the British community was matched by British facilities. An Anglican church was built in St Petersburg in 1753, an English club plus an English theatre were opened in 1770, a British naval hospital was established and the British colony came to be known as 'Little Britain on the Neva'.

The ties between the two countries continued to flourish under Catherine II in the 19th century with Russia keenly introducing British cultural and technological achievements. The Scottish architect Charles Cameron came to St Petersburg at the personal invitation of Catherine II to design improvements to her country residence the Tsarskoe Selo palace. A gallery in one of the buildings is named after him. Landscape designer James Madders created an English landscaped park in Peterhof and his colleague William Gould created the Tavrichesky Garden in the centre of St Petersburg. The Scottish architect William Hastie designed some of the unique iron bridges in the city. British engineers also installed St Petersburg's first steam engine and tram. In addition to numerous British managed factories and shops, there was even a branch of Britain's Bowlton & Co bank at 6 Admiralty Embankment and a British bookshop and reading room were a great success with the locals. The city's first English-language newspaper was named Friendship and there were a number of British charities and hospitals in the city. There was an English shop in the city that sold marmalade, shortbread and other English goods. A local newspaper report in 1851 stated, '*Now that we have a yacht club and horse racing we can honestly say English sport is here.*' The English word 'sport' was then imported into the Russian language and the British led the way in the city's athletic life, founding its first clubs for rowing, biking, track and field, tennis and football. As regular visitors to St Petersburg, John Hughes and his sons no doubt took advantage of these English facilities. By the end of the 19th century there were over 2,000 British citizens in St Petersburg. Blood ties between the English and Russian royal houses also strengthened relationships between the two countries. Tsar Alexander I was Queen Victoria's godfather and Alexander II had made an approach to wed her soon after she became queen but she chose Prince Albert instead. Alice, the granddaughter of Queen Victoria, became the last Russian empress Alexandra Fyodorovna.

The British had an important role in providing capital and technical knowledge to Russia during the 19th century, especially in the textile and paper industries. They were able to bring the most modern manufacturing techniques and skilled men to Russia and '*outstrip most of the local competition and to accumulate substantial profits*'.[54] In the 1840s and 1850s several large British owned companies were established, such as the textile businesses of James Thornton, Hubbard and Egerton plus John and Joseph Shaw. In the machinery and metallurgical sectors, names such as Carr & McPherson, Ellis & Butts, Wilkins and Isherwood were important in St Petersburg and Smith, Bromley and Williams were active in Moscow. Probably the most famous names of them all were Baird and Gascoigne.

Charles Baird was an expert in the casting of guns at the Carron Company in Glasgow and came to Russia in 1786 following a

---

54   William Blackwell – ibid

request to Carron from the Russian government to provide help with establishing a canon foundry in Kronstadt. Together with Gascoigne, he built the Baird works in Kronstadt, which was later moved to Kolpino near St Petersburg and it became extremely successful, known for its order and efficiency. Baird built the first Russian steamship, the Elizaveta with a brick chimney for a funnel. It plied between St Petersburg and Kronstadt and Baird had a ten-year monopoly which made his fortune. His son, Francis, who joined his father in Russia at the age of 17, took over the business at his father's death in 1843. The Baird works produced the dome of St Isaac's Cathedral, considered an engineering feat at the time, as well as all the iron works for the first iron bridges in St Petersburg. Several hundred skilled British workers were employed at the Baird factories. When Francis Baird died in 1864, he was followed by his son George who became head of the Baird Works. In 1871 he was granted the extraordinary honour of being confirmed by Tsar Alexander II as a hereditary Russian nobleman.

Originally from Yorkshire, Gascoigne was another engineer from the Carron iron works who travelled to Russia with Charles Baird. Whilst at Carron, he invented a new gun, called the Carronade, which was used to great effect in the Napoleonic wars. Although not as well known as Baird, Gascoigne certainly left his imprint on Russia. He was instrumental in setting up the Lugansk iron works in Ukraine (see page 60); he designed the new St Petersburg Mint and he created a new Russian unit of measure based on the inch (the distance between the top and knuckle of the thumb). He was appointed director of the Alexandrovsky Gun Works and Konchezersky Foundry with the responsibility of organising large-scale production of artillery weapons and ammunition for the Russian military. Gascoigne also taught metal casting to Russian workers and was made head of mines and a state councillor, effectively becoming a member of the Russian government. Like Baird, Gascoigne lived out the rest of his life and died in Russia in 1806.

So John Hughes was not the only British entrepreneur to have an impact on Russia in the 19th century. But he was exceptional in that he started a new business from scratch, away from the traditional centres of St Petersburg or Moscow and came under his own steam, rather than furthering an existing company's commercial expansion into the country. A wide range of British companies established themselves in Russia during this period, with textiles, mining, engineering and oil being the principal sectors of interest. They came to develop market opportunities and unlike Hughes, they mostly concentrated on those areas of the economy not controlled or influenced by the Russian state. They brought with them new technologies, investment and products and many of these companies became very profitable multi-million-pound businesses. In 1921, the British Board of Trade's register of claims following the revolution stood at over 1.7 billion roubles of which it felt at least half to be genuine.

As with the New Russia Company, British managers were employed almost exclusively to run these operations and key skilled workers were brought in initially to train local workers. The opportunities and rewards for foreign skilled workers immigrating to Russia in the second half of the 19th century were considerable but not widely appreciated. Compared with North America, Australia and later Africa, the challenges of climate, language and culture dissuaded many. But of those that did come, a high proportion stayed on beyond their initial contract, moving to more senior positions or setting up in business on their own. Barry[55] cites the example of a British man he met in Tiumen in western Siberia –

55   Herbert Barry – ibid

'I was a foreman in Glasgow seven years ago, when I had the offer of coming here. I wanted to better myself ... I have got 15,000 roubles (about £2000) in the bank ... and now I am going into building steamboats, which I mean to run on the Siberian rivers.'

It would have been almost unthinkable for such a man to accumulate this sum over the same period working in Britain. It is estimated that there were close to 6,000 British subjects in the Russian Empire at the start of the First World War with around 2,500 in St Petersburg, 600 in Moscow and the rest scattered across the country. There were extended families of the Bairds, Carrs, Gibsons and Hills that had been there for several generations but which still maintained much of their British identity. Although the British community was essentially middle-class, a fascinating mixture of professions is listed in the St Petersburg British Consulate register of births. This included amongst the fathers' professions: merchant, accountant, jockey, ringmaster, cotton mill manager, clerk, weaving manager, banker, iron moulder, cotton carder, mechanic, electrical engineer, mining engineer, foreman printer and head brewer. Although a successful and wealthy businessman, John Hughes with his humble origins probably felt more at ease in this polyglot British group than he did in London. It's clear that he had several friends in St Petersburg and his eldest son was well known in the foreign community.

The British workers that went to Hughesovka were quite a mixed bunch with a variety of skills and reasons for going. Although many were of Welsh origin, the rest came from various parts of Britain. There were engineers, miners, blast furnace men, boiler men, machinists, metal workers, masons, clerks and later men with more specialised skills arrived such as chemists, electricians and technicians. Those who stayed longer often rose up through the ranks of management. Some came simply to earn money that would allow them to return home to a better life, perhaps to marry or buy their own home. Others came because they needed work at times of depression in Britain but they were skilled workers able to earn a living anywhere and none were destitute. They were not part of the 'poor and huddled masses' so many of whom emigrated from Britain in the 19th century. Some stayed for just the period of their initial contract, usually three years, others stayed much longer with a few settling in Hughesovka and raising a family. Of the latter group, some met and married local women, others brought their wives out from Britain – not always successfully though. A few wives simply wouldn't uproot and move to distant Russia, as was probably the situation with Hughes' own wife. There is one recorded case of the wife of a Daniel Jenkins who set off from Wales in the 1890s to join her husband in Hughesovka. While sitting at the station with her trunk, she changed her mind and let the train leave without her, remaining at home to run a public house[56]. Out of the unmarried men that came, many remained single for the duration of their stay in Hughesovka though some undoubtedly had liaisons with local women and even illegitimate children. There are accounts of Russians with English surnames still in the area after the 1917 revolution who then adopted more Russian-sounding versions of their names to avoid trouble.

Probably the largest British family that lived in Hughesovka was that of David James and his wife Mary. They arrived in the early 1870s with seven children and had a further three during their time in Hughesovka, ending up with over 40 descendants born in Russia. Their eldest son married Mary Oldfield from St Petersburg whose mother had been an English tutor to the royal family. David James' first child born in Hughesovka grew up to marry Charles Perry, the son of the manager of the Krivoi Rog iron mines. Another prolific family was that of David Waters from Swansea whose wife had five children in Hughesovka.

Edwin James (no relation to David James) became a close associate

---

56   Susan Edwards – ibid

of Hughes and was the company's mineral surveyor, mining engineer and subsequently managed the company's extensive coal mines that employed more than 4,000 men, over a period of 18 years. He lived in Hughesovka for more than 30 years from 1872 to around 1904 and his daughter Evelina Probert went to the English school. She lived in Russia for 11 years (1872 to 1883) before returning home to marry. Another James was Thomas James who together with his brother Samuel was awarded a gold medal from the Tsar for saving the lives of 13 miners in the nearby Anensky colliery in 1905. Thomas owned and operated a coal mine in Hughesovka but lost everything when the revolution forced him to return to Britain.

Alexander Cameron, who we first met in Chapter Two, was born in Aberdeen in 1825 and had trained as an engineer, becoming an experienced iron foundry man. There is no record of when he first met John Hughes but it was possibly at Millwall as Cameron was certainly working in London by 1850 and three of his children were born there. Cameron moved to Ukraine in the early 1860s to work in the Lugansk ironworks and his youngest son William was born in Kharkov in 1862, When Hughes first visited Ukraine he probably contacted Cameron and asked for his help, later offering him a job as paymaster with his new company. Cameron's knowledge of the country and ironworking would have proved extremely useful to Hughes, especially in the early days and he also acted at times as Hughes' personal translator. It seems Hughes never did learn Russian and there was no modern Anglo-Russian dictionary or grammar book. The only one in print dated from 1696 and certainly wouldn't have covered the kind of specialist vocabulary needed by Hughes. As we have already seen, Cameron helped survey the Donets coal fields with George Hume and gave his report to Hughes. Cameron moved to Hughesovka with his wife Helen and their son William who had trained as a civil engineer and later helped build the Trans-Siberian Railway. William's daughter Kathleen was born in Hughesovka. When she was just one year old, the 1917 revolution forced the Cameron family to flee the country and they settled in England near Sheffield (coincidentally now the twin city of Donetsk). Cameron's brother-in-law, Frederick Loxley, apparently decided to stay on until forced a little later by his own workers to leave. They pushed him in a wheelbarrow through the works and dumped him outside the gates.

Annie Gwen Jones came out to Hughesovka in 1889 as tutor to the children of Arthur Hughes and she stayed for three years. She later recounted to her family back in Wales many stories of the happy times she had spent in Hughesovka. She was fortunate to have enjoyed a relatively privileged life with the Hughes family but during her time there she also developed a concern for the less fortunate among the Russian people. She sympathised with the calls at the time for improved social conditions as well as the poverty of the peasants, the harsh treatment of the Jews and the suppression of the Polish people. She passed on her love of Ukraine and her high moral principles to her son Gareth Jones. He was born in Wales in 1905 after her return from Hughesovka. He became a famous journalist working for the Western Mail in Wales. The stories that his mother used to tell him as a child about her life in Russia made a deep impression on him and he visited Russia several times in the early 1930s to report for his newspaper on conditions under Stalin. Jones travelled through Russia and the Ukraine and was shocked at the conditions he encountered, especially the starvation and genocide in Ukraine and general repression in Russia. Although there were many western accredited journalists in Russia at the time, none had reported on this story. Jones estimated seven to ten million people died between 1932 and 1933 and was the first to reveal to the world the true conditions experienced by millions under the rule of Stalin. He was murdered in 1935 on the eve of his 30th birthday by bandits while travelling in Inner Mongolia.

Arthur Riddle was appointed as the first Anglican chaplain at the English church in December 1902 and moved to Hughesovka from St Petersburg with his wife Mary and their four children.

This was a position created for him by John James Hughes who was godfather to the Riddle's eldest son. Arthur Riddle had been working for the English church in the St Petersburg region for several years and was known as 'Friar Tuck' due to his large girth and love of good food. Mary came from the Wishaw family who were well-established British merchants in St Petersburg and as well as being good friends of the Hughes family, their social circle included the Revillon (Whistler) family and the Carrs. Coming from St Petersburg, Mary initially found it hard to adapt to the more limited environment of Hughesovka but the family remained there until the death of Arthur in 1911. Their two sons were sent away to school in England, returning for the summer holidays. Mary was also unhappy with their initial home complaining that it was not as spacious as the family was used to in St Petersburg and the chaplaincy was later allocated a much larger house by the company. As with Arthur Riddle, not all the British workers and their families who lived in Hughesovka survived to return home. Some of their children died there, often at an early age and a few of the adults also died in the town and were also buried there. Despite the various epidemics in the Donbass, the overall death rate among the foreign community was probably marginally higher than in a comparable British town of the time but not inordinately so.

Perhaps the most famous resident of Hughesovka was the Communist leader Nikita Khrushchev who was born in 1894 in a small south Ukrainian village called Kalinovka. He was part of a large peasant family who had struggled to make a living on a small plot of land. After a couple of years' schooling, Khrushchev worked as a cow herd to supplement his family's meagre income. His father took a second job as a coal miner but despite this the family was unable to survive as farmers. So when he was 15, the family moved to Hughesovka where Khrushchev found a job initially as a farmhand then as a joiner in the factory and later in the coal mines. He worked in the Rutchenko mine, eventually becoming deputy manager. Although he was involved in the local strikes in 1914 and 1915, he was initially not very active politically. In 1917 however, at the age of 23, he decided to join the Bolsheviks, seeing this as an opportunity to advance himself and escape from his social environment. As a coal miner, he was exempt from military service and by now he was married with two children, which made him want to remain near Hughesovka. However, in 1919 he went off to join the Red Army as a political worker in the civil war, seeking to prove himself to be a loyal and useful Communist. At the end of the war, he returned home and was given the task of organizing a local Communist party.

When he arrived back in Hughesovka he found the Donbass like much of the Ukraine, suffering due to severe famine. In the chaos caused by the revolution and civil war, there was mass unemployment and great destitution and many died, including Khrushchev's wife. It was a very sad and difficult time for him but he set about restoring production in the local factories and mines. In 1921, he sent his children to live with his parents and enrolled in a mining technology school, where he developed both his engineering and political skills as well as learning how to read. After four years Khrushchev graduated and married again. In 1925 at the age of 31 he was appointed party secretary of a district near Hughesovka and gradually rose up the Communist party organization to become first secretary of the city of Moscow in 1935 and Politburo member by 1939.

Despite the difficulties surrounding his early years in Hughesovka, Khrushchev seems to have retained some fond memories of his time there. Recalling his later visit to England in his memoirs, Khrushchev commented on the long rows of little red brick houses that reminded him so much of the homes that Hughes had built for his workers in Hughesovka. In an interview with The Times newspaper in 1961 he commented favourably on Hughes, praising his fairness. Khrushchev also even claimed to

Women making horseshoes in a machine shop c.1915 *(GRO)*

Bridge building with girders from the New Russia Company *(GRO)*

The New Russia Company's works 1912 *(GRO)*

View of the town 1912 *(GRO)*

The foundry 1912 *(GRO)*

Keeping the coal moving in winter snows *(GRO)*

Hughesovka's football team

British army volunteers leaving Hughesovka in 1914 *(GRO)*

have played football for the New Russia Company's team while in Hughesovka. During negotiations with the Indian government in the 1960s to build a steel plant there, the Russians were in competition with the British. Although the Russians eventually won, Khrushchev later wrote in his memoirs, '*I knew from my childhood that the British were first class steelmen. Hughesovka, the town where I grew up, was named after the owner of the local steel factory – Hughes. The British in general have always been marvellous with technology.*'

CHAPTER TEN
Wars and Revolutions

In 1904 war broke out between Russia and Japan. This conflict grew out of the rival imperialist ambitions of the Russian and Japanese Empires over Manchuria and Korea. For many years the Russians had been seeking a warm-water port on the Pacific Ocean both as a naval base and for commercial trade. Although they had recently established the port of Vladivostok, it was only fully operational during the summer season and the Russians had their eyes on Port Arthur in Manchuria, which was free of ice all year round. Protracted negotiations between the Tsar's government and Japan had proved futile and in the face of Russian threats, the Japanese chose war rather than lose influence in the region. The war was initially popular in Russia and the outside world was surprised at Japan's decision, expecting the larger Russian forces to easily overwhelm the fledgling Japanese military. However, the Japanese consistently achieved victory over the Russians and this success dramatically transformed the balance of power in northeast Asia, causing a sober reassessment of Japan's recent arrival onto the world stage. For Russia, the defeats were not only embarrassing but brought about increased dissatisfaction with the inefficient and corrupt Tsarist government and were a major cause of the 1905 revolution.

This was the first major victory by an Eastern country over a Western one in the modern era and Japan's prestige rose greatly as it began to now be considered a modern great power. Russia suffered the loss of virtually its entire Asian and Baltic fleets as well as the Tsarist armies being held to a bloody stalemate in Mongolia and Manchuria. Just as important in the long term was Russia's resulting loss of international esteem. Germany in particular took note of the change in Russia's position. Since Russia was France's ally the loss of prestige would have a significant effect on Germany's future planning for war with France and Russia in 1914. Although Great Britain was an ally of Japan at this time and remained neutral throughout the conflict, it was almost dragged into the war inadvertently. The Russians wanted to reinforce their Asian naval forces by sending their Baltic Sea fleet around the world via the Cape of Good Hope. On October 21, 1904, while passing by the southern English coast they nearly provoked a war with Britain by firing on British fishing boats that they mistook for enemy torpedo boats. A lock of Admiral Nelson's hair was given to the Imperial Japanese Navy by the Royal Navy after the war to commemorate the victory of the 1905 Battle of Tsushima, which marked the centennial of Britain's victory over the French at Trafalgar in 1805. As with the Crimean war, the defeat by the Japanese brought about a major review of Russia's military capability as well as significant rearmament. Russia had lost two of its three naval fleets with only its Black Sea fleet remaining. This gave Russian industry a much-needed boost after several years of weak demand and the New Russia Company benefited from a rise in orders for steel.

Following the war with Japan, Russia plunged into an even more serious crisis with widespread revolution in 1905, the root causes of which had been steadily developing over the previous two decades. Following the assassination in 1881 of Tsar Alexander II by bombs thrown at his carriage while on his way to church, the new Tsar, Alexander III reacted to his father's death with harsh repression. Both the police and the Russian secret police political service (the Okhrana) took rapid and effective action to suppress the various revolutionary and democratic movements across the country. The Okhrana scattered the revolutionary groups through imprisonment, execution or exile while a few escaped to Europe. By April 1906, more than 14,000 people had been executed and 75,000 were thrown in prison, many of them Jews. Alexander III also stepped up persecution of the Jews (who had been involved in Alexander's assassination), imposing the Russian language on all minority nationalities in the empire and at the same time severely restricting the power of local government. After the assassination of Alexander II the already difficult position of Jews in Russia became untenable and around two million eventually decided to emigrate, some to Europe but mostly to North America. It was through the group that moved to Europe that Russian thinkers first came into contact with the concept of Marxism and the first Russian Marxist group was formed as early as 1884. These repressive measures amplified the existing feelings of alienation and discontent of much of the population. Underlying much of the political disquiet was a growing frustration with Russia's poor economic performance. The country's rapidly expanding population was experiencing rising unemployment, food shortages and general poverty. Although economic growth had been rapid under Tsar Alexander II it was concentrated in a few regions, chiefly around Moscow, Saint Petersburg, Ukraine and the oil fields of Baku. Roughly one third of all the capital invested was foreign and although foreign entrepreneurs were vital, there was growing resentment at their power and influence over the economy in several sectors of Russian society. There were concerns too that this process of growth was allowing the rich to become richer, while in their view the poor became poorer as cheap Russian labour was exploited.

Despite having introduced the emancipation of serfs and several other key reforms, Alexander II had been the target of several earlier assassination attempts. In the 1881 attack, an initial bomb thrown at his bullet-proof carriage (a gift from Napoleon III of France) injured his guards and bystanders but failed to harm the Tsar. However, the Tsar then made the fatal mistake of emerging from his damaged carriage whereupon a second bomb was thrown by another revolutionary, which fatally injured him.

Against this background, the 1905 revolution in Russia developed into a violent struggle that erupted across large parts of the Tsarist Empire. It was a battle against the government as well as society in general and was neither controlled nor directed by any single group. Although it had no single cause or aim, it was the culmination of decades of unrest and dissatisfaction stemming from the Tsar's autocratic rule and the slow pace of reform in Russian society. The extent and severity of the revolt were amplified by demands for national freedom from the many non-Russians within the empire, including Ukrainians. But the spark that lit the smouldering fuse was the abject failure of the Tsar's military forces in the war against the Japanese. The defeat set off a series of revolutionary reaction, sometimes by mutinous troops and at other times by revolutionary or outright terrorist groups. The abortive coup was heralded by a naval mutiny on board the battleship *Potemkin* in the Black Sea, later immortalised in a famous film of the same name by the Bolsheviks. Although put down with a blend of compromise and savagery, the revolution did increase the pace of reform in Russia, but not enough to prevent the subsequent 1917 revolution. Indeed, the Bolsheviks considered the revolution of 1905 to be a popular precursor to their own revolution.

As the labour unrest of 1905 spread to the industrial region of southern Russia, the companies were hit by a series of violent strikes and the province of Ekaterinoslav was one of the most violent and volatile areas. The violent unrest included Donbass coal miners, militant railroaders plus industrial factory workers in and around the mines, the towns and Ekaterinoslav itself. Although protest and upheaval were by no means new to the region, in 1905 the province witnessed a chain of strikes, meetings and demonstrations throughout the year culminating in December in one of the largest and most militant armed uprisings in the whole of Russia. The province also saw several destructive anti-Jewish pogroms among the hundreds that swept south Russia in October, and Hughesovka and the New Russia Company were not spared from this disorder. Although companies in south Russia were forced to call on the government for military protection for their enterprises, there was some sympathy with the underlying causes of the unrest. Industry bodies criticised the government for its poor economic policies and unfair laws as well as its failure to implement true reform. The steel companies supported calls for better treatment of workers through equality before the law, freedom of speech and protection of basic rights. There was some political opportunism in this stance, however, as the Congress of Mining Industrialists mistakenly felt that if successful, the revolt would weaken the government and allow them more influence.

After a few years of relative calm, the outbreak of the First World War In 1914 proved to be a catastrophe for Tsarist Russia. The government had not anticipated such a conflict and the country was poorly prepared for a major war. Although the embarrassing defeat by Japan nine years earlier had brought about some improvements to the nation's armed forces, the turmoil of the 1905 revolution had shaken the empire and subsequent economic and political reforms were far from complete. However, as masses of workers and peasants rallied to the Russian flag in positive mood and marched off to fight, the initial outlook for both war and national unity appeared good. But this early euphoria could only survive with victory and Russia's hopes were dashed very early in the war. At the battles around Tannenberg in September 1914, the Germans destroyed two entire Russian armies (more than 250,000 men killed or wounded) and the survivors fled from the field. The leadership of the Russian senior officer corps during the First World War was appalling and the two commanders of the army were not even on speaking terms. Although the Russians regrouped and had some later battle successes, they were relatively few and by 1917, much of the Tsarist army had literally been bled to death. Critics of the regime were asking whether Russia's misfortunes – including 1,700,000 military dead and 5,000,000 wounded – were the result of stupidity or treason. The regime seemed careless of such appalling losses and the Tsar said it was an honour to lose so many men in defence of their allies. By then the Tsarist situation was hopeless and beyond saving. The mounting battlefield losses and resultant rising unrest were simply too much and the Romanov aristocracy and its government collapsed, plunging Russia into civil war.

With the onset of the First World War, industrial production expanded further to meet the demands of the war effort. Although the war initially brought great benefit to the Russian manufacturing sector, it was not welcomed by many industrialists who recognised the country's lack of preparation. As the war effort gathered pace in 1915 and existing stocks of munitions rapidly dwindled, existing armaments manufacturers (mostly state controlled) were unable to meet rising military needs. To boost supply, the government let large numbers of contracts, often at very favourable prices, to a wide range of engineering companies – both large and small. Businesses like the New Russia Company quickly switched production to munitions and for the first time, the company started manufacturing armaments, primarily high-explosive artillery shells. The government also intervened directly in the iron and steel markets by fixing prices and belatedly allocating resources for defence contractors. Overall industrial production in Russia rose rapidly; by 1916 it was some 20% higher than in 1913, with an even higher ratio going to armaments. But it could not keep pace with demand and was an important contributor to Russia's lack of success in the war.

The outbreak of war seemed to come as something of a surprise to the British community in the Donbass. This was largely due to the convoluted process that led to war and the initial secrecy surrounding Russia's mobilisation. Elizabeth Perry in Krivoi Rog wrote to her sister in August 1914 that '*the war was started so suddenly no one knew anything about it*'.[57] Along with so many other British expatriates around the world, some of the young British workers in Hughesovka volunteered to return home to join the army. A photograph from November 1914 shows 11 of them at the railway station holding a Union Jack and several of them looked quite Russian in their hats and greatcoats. As in Britain, there was a general expectation that the war would not last long and they would be back within a year. But of course the war dragged on and not all survived. Then at the onset of the Russian Revolution in 1917, most British families left Hughesovka and made their way home. In a few cases, usually where a British worker had married a Russian, the wives and children remained. But cruelly, the subsequent civil wars prevented both their husbands who had volunteered for the British army from returning and the families in Russia from leaving for several years. William Clark, who went to fight in 1914, leaving his Russian born wife and daughter behind, was unable to return for 11 years. But by then, it was clear there was no future left in Hughesovka for them and they were forced to leave. A few of the British community did stay on however and some of their descendants are living in today's Donetsk.

By early 1917, the seeds of revolution were clearly growing in almost every section of society – the defeated, disillusioned armed forces, the hungry and disgruntled working masses, the impoverished peasants, some landowners dissatisfied with agrarian policies, members of the liberal intelligentsia, various persecuted minorities plus a wide range of merchants and industrialists who felt impotent in the face of the government's failure to modernise. Through

---

57   Susan Edwards – ibid

a combination of a lack of understanding of the seriousness of the situation, insensitivity to his nation's needs and overall indecision, The Tsar lost control and the respect of his people. Talk of revolution and open sedition were everywhere. The first attempt at revolution occurred in February 1917, the so-called 'bloodless revolution' which brought about the abdication of Tsar Nicholas II and the formation of a provisional government under Prime Minister Kerensky.

However, the revolution found the foreign entrepreneurs and industrialists largely unprepared for the path that it followed. Initially, it was hard for them to understand the Bolsheviks and take them seriously. A feeling of desperation arose as they found themselves in a world of turmoil and instability, with a dysfunctional government and unable to resist the rising tide of worker militancy. Lack of agreement between industry and the provisional government about labour relations and the increased level of state control introduced for the war economy only worsened the situation. Each side blamed the other for the lack of a co-ordinated approach and forceful leadership. In southern Russia, companies were forced to concede higher wages and an eight-hour day. As attacks on managers and other key employees rose, the industrialists clamoured for government forces to restore labour discipline and protect their plants. But internal feuds in the provisional government and disagreements among various industry factions ensured a lack of any forceful action. Industry's failure to co-ordinate a unified national response to deal with the provisional government and the workers' unrest hastened their downfall. Confronted with mass strikes, falling production and reduced revenues, they remained immobile like rabbits caught in the headlights of a car. As the revolution moved to its peak, workers seized managers and began to dismantle some of the factories. The owners ordered their factories to be closed and the workers thrown out into the street. In the midst of such chaos, total collapse of order was both inevitable and imminent.

In Hughesovka there appears to have been little sympathy with the revolution among the British community. Despite the earlier good working relations and friendships between them and the Russians plus the fact that most of the British were working class, a growing atmosphere of suspicion and enmity now prevailed. So it's hardly surprising that one of the British wives wrote, '*The Revolution was abhorrent to my husband and he decided that our family should leave Russia for good.*' The collapse of the Tsarist regime in March 1917 plunged Hughesovka into prolonged chaos and civil war. Groups of workers, sometimes armed, roamed the streets clashing with police and Cossack troops. Leah Steel, wife of Thomas, the works manager, and one of the British wives still in Hughesovka later recalled the situation they faced –

'*In our area mobs of people roamed around claiming everything as their own. At one time a mob came and demanded to see my husband, who came out and asked them what they wanted. They said "You have a lot of silver in the house, and it now belongs to us." He replied, "You people presented it to me as a gift on my 25th anniversary, if you want it back, take it." They ... then said, "It is true, it is yours, please keep it." They also wanted to take over our beautiful gardens, about 2 acres... but when they were asked who would take care of it, they said no, please keep it, it would soon be ruined as a public garden. From then on they gave us no trouble.*' [58]

With life and property under threat, the more sensible foreigners in Hughesovka, like others across Russia, quickly fled the country in 1917 with most of the remainder leaving in 1918. In Krivoi Rog all seemed peaceful but news of the serious disturbances in Hughesovka and other nearby towns persuaded the Perry family to also leave in 1917. They returned to Britain, fully expecting to be back running the company's iron mines within the year and leaving their house and pets to be taken care of by their housekeeper. In

---

58   Susan Edwards – ibid

mid-June 1917, James Leask the chaplain at the English church in Hughesovka, had similarly made up his mind to leave immediately. He hastily copied out the entries from his church registers onto blank pages then cut them out and sent them to the British Consul in Odessa. The chaplaincy in Hughesovka was never re-established, though the Gibraltar Diocesan Gazette defiantly continued to list it – and the service times – until well into the 1920s. Both Leask and the registers made it home, the latter in the British Consul's baggage, when he quit the ravaged port of Odessa. They and a photograph are all that now remains of the English Church of Hughesovka.

Armed workers (now called the Red Guards) tried to seize control of the town in November 1917 by disarming the local police of the Provisional Government. The Bolsheviks then organized a mixed force of 3,000 men and with the help of other Red forces in the region captured the town. Hughesovka's resources were immediately plundered as they started shipping out by rail quantities of coal and equipment seized from the town's various factories to other parts of Russia. Their control of the region and Hughesovka was short-lived, as German forces moving into Ukraine occupied the town in April 1918.

There is strong evidence that Joseph Stalin paid a brief visit to South Wales in 1917 to raise funds and support for the Russian Revolution. The Welsh writer John Summers claimed to have been told about this during a visit to Hughesovka (by then the city of Donetsk) in 1975 and it was also mentioned in the British newspaper The Sunday Times.

For the British families trying to flee the Bolsheviks and escape from Russia in 1917 there was a difficult choice to be made. In the early 20th century, the normal route to and from Hughesovka for the British was across the English Channel and then overland by train through Germany, on to Warsaw and then into Russia. With the outbreak of the First World War, this route was closed. There were now two possible ways home – either south to one of the Black Sea ports and then out by ship across the Mediterranean or north to St Petersburg by train and on to Scandinavia and thence to Britain by ship. Both routes were full of uncertainty and danger. Although the Black Sea ports were much closer to Hughesovka, the southern Ukraine was in a state of chaos as fighting raged between the Red and White Russian armies. After that, exiting the Black Sea through the Dardanelle Straights would be highly dangerous as they were controlled by the Turks who were allied to the Germans. In addition, Turkish 'U' boats patrolled the Black Sea, attacking commercial as well as military vessels. The journey north to St Petersburg was longer and unpredictable but the trains were still running, albeit unreliably. Once there, although the city was the centre of the Bolshevik revolution and therefore danger-ous, the British were still allies of the Russians and so it should be relatively easy to cross into Finland or Sweden. However, the last leg of the journey by steamer from Norway across the North Sea to Britain would also very risky due to the presence of the German navy. Neither route was without significant dangers and this may explain why some of the British families in Hughesovka (and elsewhere in Russia) did not leave as early as they might have. In the end, it seems most families chose the northern route as being the safer option and the Steels, Camerons, Wilkins, Perrys and many others left Hughesovka this way. The Royal Navy sent ships to Bergen in Norway to escort the British steamboats on the journey home. The dangers from attack by the Germans were very real and one group of British evacuees described watching from the port as one of the transports was sunk off shore. Although sev-eral thousand escaped this way in 1917 and 1918, there were still sizeable numbers of British and other foreigners trapped in Russia. The Bolsheviks, now that they were more firmly in control of St Petersburg, had clamped down on those trying to leave. As a result, in 1919 discussions were held in Scandinavia between the Russian and British governments which eventually agreed a deal that let the remaining British out in exchange for allowing Russians out of Britain. Many of the British in St Petersburg came out through Finland and the Finns later set up a holding camp to quarantine refugees as a protection against typhus, which was spreading fast in Russia. They were often half starved and arrived with nothing more than the clothes on their backs. A trickle of refugees continued to arrive back in Britain through the early 1920s but a few stayed on, mainly Russian women and their children who had married British men and a charity was set up in Britain to try to look after them. Little is known about the fate of those who decided to remain but records of the relief committee suggest that some were still dependent on charity as late as 1930. The turmoil of the Russian Civil War and the ensuing Soviet clampdown on contact with the West resulted in this British diaspora largely disappearing from the pages of history.

With the abdication of the Tsar in early 1917, Ukraine made its first tentative steps towards independence with the formation of a provisional government, the Central Rada in Kiev. When the Bolsheviks staged their revolution in October, the Central Rada formally declared independence and Ukraine, after two centuries, briefly became a free country. But the country was not fully ready for independence and it rapidly fragmented. With no effective central government, the Ukraine soon became a centre of violent conflict that was to last for several years. Various factions struggled for power – Ukrainian independence supporters, Reds (Russian Bolsheviks), Whites (Russian supporters of the monarchy), Blacks (anarchists), Greens (independent peasant partisan forces) with intervention and support from different foreign forces (initially German and Austrian troops and then later Anglo-French forces). The Donbass became one of the most fiercely contested territories in the emerging Russian Civil War and between 1918 and 1921 it changed hands several dozen times. There was considerable fighting in and around Hughesovka with the first engagements between the Red Guards and White Russian forces occurring as early as December 1917. The reason for the bitterness and duration of this struggle was simple – the tremendous economic power of the Donbass. At the end of the First World War, the region had been producing 87% of Russia's coal output, 76% of its pig iron, 57% of its steel, more than 90% of its coke, over 60% of its soda and mercury as well important manufactured and agricultural goods. It was with good reason that Vladimir Lenin, the leader of Russian Bolsheviks, then described the Donbas as not merely '*an indispensable area*' but '*a region, without which the entire construction of socialism would just be a piece of wishful thinking*'.

The southern Ukraine had been largely under the control of anti-Bolshevik Cossack forces from as early as November 1917. Despite having a large industrialised population, the region had not fully accepted the Bolshevik proletarian revolution, much to their frustration. Ambitions for Ukrainian independence together with a growing anti-Russian peasant partisan group plus the broad mix of other nationalities generated different ideas about the path of revolution here. Also the German occupation from March to November 1918 followed by the arrival of Anglo-French, Greek and Polish forces kept the coastal Ukraine relatively free from Bolshevik influence and enabled a large White Army, which at its peak grew to some 250,000 men to become established. In January 1918, the Bolsheviks launched an offensive in the northern Ukraine and advanced on Kiev. Almost immediately, the fourth Congress of the Donbas Soviets proclaimed the creation of a separate Donetsk-Krivoi Rog Republic joining the Soviet Russia. But faced with advancing German troops, the Bolsheviks had to dismantle the Donetsk-Krivoi Rog government and retreated from Ukraine entirely in April 1918. With the capitulation of Germany in November 1918, their forces withdrew from Ukraine and the brief period of relative calm under German control in Hughesovka and the rest of the Donbass came to an end. The previous chaos and civil war rapidly returned to Ukraine and as the line of fighting ebbed and flowed, there were many civilian casualties with each side guilty of hanging and shooting opponents with several such incidents in Hughesovka. The officially restored Ukrainian People's Republic was unable to cope with the mounting economic and social problems and failed to establish an effective administration. The Bolsheviks quickly launched a new offensive advancing into the Donbas in December 1918 at the same time as the Russian Whites' southern army had entered the region, moving up from the Crimea. The Whites under General Denikin gradually pushed back the Bolshevik forces and boosted by their success launched an advance towards Moscow in the summer of 1919. Overstretched logistically and increasingly meeting stiffer resistance from Red Army troops, the offensive then stalled and collapsed less than 200 miles from the Kremlin. Thereafter, the Bolsheviks steadily regained the upper hand, forcing the remnants of the White Army back into the Crimea where they held on until November 1920.

With final defeat now inevitable, some 140,000 people escaped to Turkey in a huge sea-borne evacuation whilst many others sought refuge in Georgia and Poland. By 1921, the Donbas and most of the pre-war Ukrainian territories were under firm Bolshevik control but the cost in terms of loss of life, emigration and economic and social disruption were enormous. When the economic collapse reached rock bottom in 1921, Russia's industrial output amounted to only 12% of the pre-war level. The Bolsheviks printed vast sums of money to finance their operations, resulting in a collapse of the rouble. By 1921, the Russian currency had devalued so much that it took more than 20,000 roubles to buy a pound of butter and by 1923 the price had risen to 10,000,000 roubles! In the Ukraine, any remaining nationalist tendencies were ruthlessly crushed in a series of purges that saw millions killed or exiled to Siberia, especially the Cossacks and the remnants of the Tatars. The dream of an independent Ukraine ended with the triumph of the Bolsheviks and the founding of the Ukrainian Soviet Socialist Republic in 1922.

The Ukraine was once again a conquered province ruled directly by Russia.

British forces became involved in the civil war towards the end of 1918 and saw action in several parts of Russia. In the Ukrainian theatre, British army, navy and air force units were all in operation supporting the White Army and other anti-Bolshevik groups. The army and naval units were primarily there to provide logistical assistance. The British and French supplied the White forces in Russia with some 150 tanks, around half of which were the Mark V which had entered service during the First World War in July 1918 and proved to be extremely effective in the last battles of the war. Most of these tanks were allocated to the White Army in southern Russia. The first combat deployment of these tanks took place on May 22nd 1919 when three Mark V tanks took part in an attack on a village near Hughesovka. But the Whites failed to fully utilise these superior new weapons in frontline attacks, contributing to their eventual defeat. As the Bolsheviks gradually consolidated their control in Russia, most of these tanks were captured and adapted for use by the Red Army, some remaining in service into World War II.

The RAF had a more active fighting role during the civil war with units flying operations from several bases in southern Ukraine and the Crimea. They had a training mission at Taganrog and a forward base in Kharkov and even acquired a Russian railway train to move their equipment from base to base as the fighting fluctuated around them. Flying a mix of Sopwith Camels and De Havilland DH 9s, they flew in support of the White forces as well as direct attacks on Red Army positions. They finally handed over their remaining aircraft to the Whites in April 1920 and were evacuated. The British also tried more subversive methods to destabilise the Bolshevik regime. Robert Lockhart, the consul general in Russia prior to the revolution, was persuaded to return in 1918 as head of a special mission. Working with the British intelligence agent,

Sidney Reilly, attempts were made to overthrow the Bolshevik government. Lockhart was arrested by the Russian police and imprisoned under sentence of death but he was later released in exchange for a Russian spy captured by the British.

Following the execution of the Tsar and many other members of the Romanov family, the British government drew up a plan to try to evacuate any remaining members of the royal family and their entourage that could reach the Crimea. HMS *Marlborough* under Captain Johnson was dispatched from Constantinople on April 4th 1919 with orders to sail to Yalta to carry out a rescue. The French government had promised to participate in this mission but pulled out at the last minute. Captain Johnson carried a letter from Alexandra, the British Queen Mother to her sister, the Dowager Empress Marie of Russia, urging her to leave Russia and escape the Bolsheviks. Alexandra explained that HMS *Marlborough* had been sent to bring Empress Marie and any members of the Imperial royal family with her to England. When HMS *Marlborough* arrived in Yalta on April 7th 1919, one of the British naval officers on board was First Lieutenant Francis Pridham. He was appointed temporary ADC to Empress Marie and her entourage during the evacuation and for their journey into exile in England. He recorded the dramatic events during the few days that the *Marlborough* was in Yalta; his subsequent memoirs and the following is an extract from his book -

'*The news from up country was serious, the Bolsheviks having overcome the feeble resistance offered in the northern Crimea were now advancing rapidly southwards. Refugees were streaming into Yalta and on to the pier in ever increasing numbers, seeking safety. Soon a state of chaos reigned amongst this throng of terrified and distraught people. Children became separated from their parents and husbands from their wives and it is doubtful whether some of these unfortunate creatures ever met again. Many arrived on the pier with no other possessions than the clothes they wore. I saw one family arrive in such a state of utter panic that on reaching the harbour they jumped out of their motor car and dashed down the pier leaving the engine of the car still running. On that quay there were enough abandoned cars to provide at least one for every officer in the ship.*

On 11th April 1919 our promise to Her Majesty The Empress Marie had been fulfilled, the evacuation of Yalta was complete and HMS Marlborough could sail for Constantinople. We had then on board twenty members of the Imperial family, including two small children, and in addition twenty five ladies and gentlemen of the suites of Her Majesty, the Grand Duchess Xenia and the Grand Dukes Nicholas and Peter. Maids, servants and others added a further thirty six to the number for whom accommodation, of a kind, had been found on board. I estimated that by the time we sailed that day, in addition to our passengers, we were carrying some two hundred tons of luggage.

All that morning the Empress had been receiving the many who came on board to seek her help or to say goodbye; there was no more now that she could do for them, but up to the last moment she was deeply concerned for those who could not accompany her in the Marlborough. In the afternoon the ship, unheralded and without escort, moved silently from the anchorage off Yalta and headed into the mist of the Black Sea. Our passengers stood for long on deck gazing astern with full hearts as the beautiful coastline of the Crimea faded from their view. We did not know it at the time, but with our departure all members of the Imperial Romanov family then alive had left Russia forever, and the dynasty, which came into power in 1613, was ended.' [59]

Shortly before the evacuation at Yalta was completed by HMS *Marlborough*, a British sloop embarked about 400 of the Imperial Guard, mostly officers, who had collected at Yalta, for transport to Sevastopol. Empress Marie was brought to England, where she initially lived with her sister, Alexandra, and later in accommodation

---

59   Sir Francis Pridham – Close of a Dynasty, 1956

provided by the British royal family until her death in 1960. Francis Pridham was later given the Order of St Stanislas by the Dowager Empress. HMS *Marlborough* was subsequently also involved in the evacuation of the White Army's General Denikin from Sebastopol to Malta in April 1920.

CHAPTER ELEVEN
The Legacy of John Hughes and the New Russia Company

According to Albert Einstein, the longevity of an idea is generally correlated with its worth: '*truth is what stands the test of experience*'.

To start considering Hughes' legacy, let us look at two truths. First, after declining during the period of the Russian civil war, by 1926 Hughesovka's population had reached 174,000 – a spectacular increase in just a few years. Second, the Donetsk region is now the most densely populated region in Ukraine and the city itself has a population of over one million. Without Hughes and the business he established in Hughesovka, it is highly unlikely that either the town or the region would have developed the way they did. Hughes' immediate legacy then was the viability of the New Russia Company and the vitality of Hughesovka, which is well illustrated by the rapid rise in population once the troubles of the Bolshevik revolution and civil war were over. But his legacy goes far beyond these two simple facts. Hughes was an innovator – technically, commercially and socially – introducing a pace and direction of change not previously seen in Russia that ushered in a new type of industrialised workforce and urban culture based on a modern, well-run business.

In terms of technical innovation, Hughes was the first to use coke in the metallurgical process in the Russian Empire and the first to demonstrate in Russia the benefits of large-scale, integrated production, using modern methods and equipment, supported by investment in steam power. He also made significant investments to improve production quality, especially in the company's analytical laboratories. Hughes' technical knowledge and skills were exceptional and he was sometimes dismissive of the abilities of the Russians sent by the government to supervise his work or assist him. He *'loved to describe their amazement at the results he attained in steel-making by rule of thumb and eye alone — watching the colours of the molten mass and seizing the exact moment to withdraw it from the furnace — an accomplishment their text-books and college training had failed to impart'*. [60] Hughes was also an innovator and leader (at least as far as Russia was concerned) in the areas of labour relations, training and safety. Despite some early problems he adapted his approach and methods, achieving a more stable and loyal workforce with better skills and a safer work environment than other industrialists of the time in Russia. From his correspondence with the government, he seems to have been very committed to meeting his original obligations by training local workers and providing housing for them. Thousands of peasants were taught a wide variety of working professions at Hughes' company together with an important cadre of skilled Russian managers that contributed to the country's further industrial development in the 20th century.

Although his company was eventually surpassed in some areas by new companies that followed his trail-blazing methods, without Hughes' perseverance and determination to succeed where others had failed, the industry in Ukraine would not have developed in the way that it did. Hughes' undoubted interest in the overall development and success of the coal and metallurgical industry in Russia helped to encourage not only others to emulate his lead but also

---

60 John Baddeley – ibid

the government in its support for the sector. It was his dedication and persistence that laid the foundations for the transition of the Donetsk region and ultimately the whole of southern Ukraine from a rural backwater into a major industrial centre in the 20ᵗʰ century.

Commercially, Hughes was also an innovator in Russia as well as an astute negotiator and a ruthless competitor for both other Russian companies as well as foreign imports. Hughes was no absentee landlord leaving the running of the company to rent men and living handsomely off the profits elsewhere. He was a 'hands on' manager, intimately involved with the company and its business to the very end of his life. Indeed, it is believed that when Hughes died he was discussing the potential sale of pig iron to St Petersburg and the export of coal via the Black Sea – both of these to compete with British exports. He demonstrated the need for and benefits of sustained profits, carefully using these to grow and develop his business. When appropriate, he was not afraid to use marginal pricing as a weapon to gain additional business or enter new markets. Hughes worked intelligently within the Russian system, recognising the importance of government contacts and influential friends but remaining independent and totally focused on his core business activities. Hughes' sense of modern capitalism and innate commercial nous meant that his approach to business in Russia was different and it is no surprise that his methods and profits were carefully studied by other new enterprises. He demonstrated the advantages of integrated, large-scale production and the benefits for the company in controlling its own coal and iron mines and rail systems for transport.

Apart from the undeserved Soviet criticism of Hughes as being solely interested in profit to the detriment of his workers, the main adverse comments about him and the New Russia Company concern working conditions and various social issues in the town of Hughesovka. Simply put, the debate centres on whether Hughes' legacy in this area was good or bad. Did he lead the way and do enough to provide a decent standard of living and healthy environment for all his workers as well as the other residents in the town? Inevitably, comparisons can be drawn and figures quoted to support either case but the truth lies somewhere in between. Certainly in Soviet times, when Hughes was vilified (if he was acknowledged at all), the picture painted of Hughesovka was very critical. As we have seen, there was also criticism of Hughes and the town in several contemporary official reports and by various visitors to Hughesovka at the time. There is no doubt that the town was dirty, smoky and unhealthy and that working conditions for many of the miners were dreadful. Yet at the same time, the overall weight of comments about Hughes by those who really knew him seem to indicate that he cared very strongly about the lives and working conditions of his employees.

To fully answer the question about his legacy in the social sphere, we need to put Hughes and the town into context. How did it compare with similar settlements of that time in Russia ,or indeed elsewhere, and could Hughes or the company have done more or acted differently to improve conditions in the town? Despite the criticisms, at virtually every stage in its development through the 19th century, Hughesovka appears to have been ahead of comparable towns in Russia. With no existing settlement to build on initially, the company had to construct and fund everything, which inevitably put a greater strain on both resources and management. Although the development of Hughesovka was integral to the long-term success of the company, this always had to be balanced against the demands of the business in terms of management time and financial resources. Still, Hughes succeeded in providing decent company housing for most of his workers in the earlier years with the choice later of places to rent or buy on affordable terms with a steadily improving range of social services and facilities. In doing so, he largely overcame the transient peasant worker problem in the Donbass, achieving relatively early on a stable workforce which then developed into a homogeneous urban population.

Evidence of the early success of Hughes' policies can be seen by comparing the levels of itinerant peasant workers. The typical pattern in the Donbass during the mid 1870s was for 60% to 70% of miners to return to their villages in the summer to work the fields. At the New Russia Company's mines, however, this percentage was halved. Clearly there were a combination of factors involved but Hughes' policies towards housing, pay, healthcare and safety must have been important in both recruiting and stabilising the workforce. The fact that after the early years Hughes was never short of workers, underlines the success of his policies and the relative attractions of Hughesovka. As other large companies set up in south Russia, there were ample alternative employment opportunities. Those managers that eventually followed Hughes' lead in the social sphere found their companies achieved similar benefits. The success of Hughes' housing policy was echoed by the director of a nearby large mine that later followed the same approach: *'after I introduced the system of improving housing and all other aspects of the miners' lives, the result was that we were never short of workers'.*[61] Hughes' achievements in this respect are all the more remarkable since before arriving in Ukraine he had no experience of building or running a town and all the services that go with it.

In earlier chapters we looked in detail at various elements of the terms of employment of Hughes' workers as well as their general living conditions. In virtually every case, the situation of the New Russia Company workers was better than elsewhere, whether pay rates, the absence of truck shops and exorbitant loan rates, training, safety, healthcare, fewer child workers, jobs for the injured, widowed and old, quantity and choice of housing or social amenities. This industry-leading package helped the company to avoid much of the bad industrial relations and strikes that plagued many of Hughes' competitors. Although two separate classes of workers evolved in Hughesovka, those in the factory and the miners,

---

61 Theodore Friedgut – ibid

with differing levels of pay and housing, this was not dissimilar to the rest of the country and reflected the changing social environment developing in Russia at the time. Despite its imperfections, we have to assume, therefore, that as a place to live and work, Hughesovka was at least as attractive as other locations in Russia at the time. The fact that so many peasants who came initially for work then chose to settle in Hughesovka with their families appears to confirm this view. It also seems to have been no worse than similar industrial towns in Britain during their equivalent stages of industrial development. The factory workers' housing shown in the photos we have of Hughesovka compares well with the city tenements and back-to-back Victorian terraced slums so dominant in British industrial towns of the time. The same can be said regarding the level of social facilities and amenities. Many British towns had similar issues to Hughesovka relating to a lack of mains water, sewage systems or electricity supply until well into the 20th century; pollution, ill health and cholera outbreaks were also not solely Donbass problems. The overall weight of evidence indicates that Hughes was well respected by his workforce and the town's residents. Although in Soviet times the name of John Hughes was intentionally obscured, according to older residents who were around at the time, much of the population obstinately continued to call their city Hughesovka, ignoring the name Stalino for many years.

Following the death of Hughes in 1889, one of the St Petersburg financial newspapers on reporting this event paid him an interesting compliment. It said, '*English by origin, he was Russian in his soul, and we may boldly say that he desired Russia's industrial success as passionately as any Russian.*' [62] This comment shows the high regard in which Hughes was held at the time in Russia and the admiration for the way in which he had fervently espoused the cause of Russian industrialisation. When Hughes first established his company, he

---

62 TH Friedgut – ibid

no doubt intended to build a modern iron works that would allow him to exploit the opportunities available in a profitable way and he pursued this objective with an amazing vigour and commitment. But it is highly unlikely that taking a leading role in the industrial development of Russia was initially part of his thinking. However, at some point this changed as his New Russia Company increasingly led the field and Hughes found himself in the position of being able to help fellow industrialists as well as lobbying and influencing government. Of course there was an element of self-interest in this – his business would do better in an economy that was doing well – but there was more to Hughes' approach than that. Probably unique among the many foreign industrialists of his period in Russia, Hughes was genuinely interested in the cause of Russia's industrial development and actively sought to encourage and cajole others in his way of thinking.

As we have already noted, during the course of the 19th century the Russian Empire had gone from being a leading world exporter of iron to being a major importer. On the eve of Hughes' arrival in Ukraine, the state of Russia's metallurgical industry had recently been comprehensively assessed by Herbert Barry. [63] He had worked for three years as a director of the large Russian Vuiksa ironworks near Nizhny Novgorod, which was then government owned but under British management and had the opportunity to visit many of the iron and coal producers in the country at that time. Whilst noting the very considerable resources of the Russian Empire, he identified many of the problems that had led to the industry's relative decline in world trade. He describes the low levels of entrepreneurship, investment generally and especially in new technology, technical knowledge and training as well as highlighting the poor management, corruption and theft, continued use of wood for iron smelting rather than coal plus the high protective tariffs leading to inflated domestic prices. Yet despite these problems, the Russian

---

63   Herbert Barry – Russian Metallurgical Works, 1870

iron and coal industry was transformed over the course of the next 20 years. Why did this occur and what was the catalyst? Clearly the Tsarist government's recognition of the problems was an important step in the right direction but it was not enough. Despite the growth in domestic demand for iron rails (and coal), Russian industrialists were unable or unwilling to expand production. It was largely thanks to Hughes and his company that this transformation occurred and he became the touchstone for government and other industrialists to follow. He was the right man in the right place at the right time.

The achievements of Hughes in Hughesovka became not only the model for others to follow but also exemplified the way in which industrial capitalism in Russia could successfully develop in the late 19th century. Prior to the arrival of Hughes, the Russian government had been unsuccessful in trying to develop the resources of southern Ukraine. The opportunity of turning this region into a world-class heavy industrial centre was made reality by Hughes not the Russians. His strategic decision to link by rail the Krivoi Rog iron mines with the coal of the Donbass and then on to the coast of the Azov Sea, set the scene for the region to become a major industrial and manufacturing base in the 20th century. Lenin's statement that described the Donbass as not merely 'an indispensable area' but 'a region, without which the entire construction of socialism would just be a piece of wishful thinking' shows how important it was to the Bolsheviks. The achievements and success of Hughes, his sons and fellow British workers were largely ignored in Britain at the time. Given the strong commercial and cultural links between Britain and Russia, it is odd that this substantial British-owned company remained out of the spotlight. The location of Hughesovka, far from the main Russian centres of St Petersburg and Moscow would partly explain this. Also Hughes was no self-publicist and although he returned to visit Britain frequently for both business and pleasure, he seems to have kept a low profile. Perhaps the fact that he had settled in Russia and later competed with British coal and steel exports did not endear him to politicians and businessmen in his home country. It is interesting that when Nikita Khrushchev first visited Britain in the 1950s and had lunch at Chequers with James Griffiths, the first-ever Secretary of State for Wales, he asked the question '*Who was John Hughes?*' Griffiths was unable to answer, sadly knowing nothing of this great Welshman.

John Hughes' contributions to industrialising and modernising Russia are remarkable and his achievements stand comparison with many better-known industrialists of the Victorian era. His tangible legacy is a thriving city and one of the world's largest industrial regions. Less tangible but just as important in today's world is the example he provides as a person of integrity, courage and determination plus an illustration of what can be achieved regardless of education and background. John Hughes' ideas have stood the test of time and experience and we can now appreciate their true worth as well as the outstanding man that he undoubtedly was.

Despite his vilification by the Soviets, John Hughes outlived them and in 2004 he made a return to the town he had founded after an absence of more than 100 years. A monument to him was erected by the city on the principal street of Donetsk near the technical university. This suitably larger-than-life statue shows him robustly wielding a heavy hammer placed on an anvil. This detail is not accidental, as the smithy was the first building that Hughes erected before the construction of his iron works in the desolate Ukrainian steppe. It seems very fitting that Hughes continues to look out over the legacy he created.

BIBLIOGRAPHY & ARCHIVE SOURCES

Documentary Sources Relating to Ukraine in Repositories in the UK: Compiled by Janet M. Hartley, London, 1993-1994.

The National Archives, Kew, Richmond, Surrey TW9 4DU

Glamorgan Record Office, County Hall, Cathays Park, Cardiff CF1 3NE

Donetsk Central Library and Archives, Donetsk, Ukraine

Albov, Alexander. Recollections of Pre-Revolutionary Russia, The Bancroft Library Berkeley, California 1986

Baddeley, John Russia in the Eighties, Longmans, London 1921

Balcon, Sarah. John Hughes of Yuzovka, Britain-USSR No 89, September 1991

Barry, Herbert. Russian Metallurgical Works, London 1870

Barry, Herbert, Russia in 1870, Wyman & Sons, London 1871

Black & Macraild. Nineteenth Century Britain, Palgrave Macmillan

Blackwell, William. The Beginnings of Russian Industrialisation, Princeton University Press, 1968

Bowen, EG. John Hughes (Yuzovka) University of Wales Press, 1978

Bromley, Jonathon. Russia 1848-1917, Heinemann

Buchanan, Meriel. Recollections of Imperial Russia, Hutchinson & Co, 1923

Clark, TE, A Guide to Merthyr Tydfil and The Traveller's Companion, 1848

Cross, Anthony. By the Banks of the Neva, Cambridge University Press

Edwards, Susan. Hughesovka, Glamorgan Record Office, 1992

Edwards, HS. The Russians at Home and Abroad, WH Allen, London 1879

Edwards, W. Merthyr Tydfil in 1877, HW Southey & Sons Ltd, 1934

Entrepreneurship in Imperial Russia and the Soviet Union – Princeton University Press 1983

Friedgut, Theodore. Iusovka and Revolution Vol. 1, Princeton University Press 1989

Friedgut, Theodore. John Hughes of Iuzovka, Llafur, 1991

Gatrell, Peter. The Tsarist Economy 1850-1917, Batsford

Hayman, Richard, Working Iron in Merthyr Tydfil, 1989

Hume, George. Thirty Five Years in Russia, Simpkin, Marshall & Co., London 1914

Joubert, Carl. Russia As It really Is, Eveleigh Nash, London 1904

Karttunen, Marie-Louise. English Merchants in Imperial Russia, University of Helsinki paper 2005

Knight, Samuel. John Hughes & Yusovka, Planet Vol. 21, 1974

McKay, John. Pioneers for Profit, University of Chicago Press, 1970

Norman, Sir Henry. All the Russias, Charles Scribner, New York, 1902

Paustovsky, Konstantin. Slow Approach of Thunder, Harvill Press, 1964

Pridham, Sir Francis, Close of a Dynasty, Allan Wingate, 1956

Rieber, AJ. Merchants & Entrepreneurs in Imperial Russia, University of North Carolina Press

Wallace, Sir Donald Mackenzie. Russia on the Eve of Revolution, Random House, New York, 1961

Westwood, JN. John Hughes & Russian Metallurgy, Economic History Review, 1965 Vol. 17

Index

Guern, Marjor General 27, 39, 43, 153
Guest family 7

Hendrikoff, Count Etienne 86
HMS Marlborough 199, 200, 201
Hughes, Albert 162, 163
Hughes, Arthur 135, 140, 170, 180
Hughes, Ivor 164, 165, 172
Hughes, John James 162, 163, 181
Hume, George 29, 31, 32, 80, 167, 179

industrial revolution ix, 1, 2, 5, 21, 85, 154

James, David 178
James, Edwin 178
James, Thomas 92, 179
Japan 74, 165, 184, 185, 188
Jews 60, 127, 128, 144, 180, 186
Jones, Annie Gwen 135, 142, 180
Jones, Gareth 180

Katherine II 61
Kharkov 29, 30, 32, 49, 59, 81, 88, 92, 94, 99, 146, 151, 153, 179, 198
Khrushchev, Nikita 181, 182, 210
Kiev 55, 58, 59, 128, 143, 146, 151, 195, 196
Kochubei, Prince Serge 29, 31, 32, 34, 154
Kolpino 28, 175
Krivoi Rog 48, 86, 87, 88, 122, 145, 178, 190, 192, 196, 209
Kronstadt iii, 18, 21, 25, 26, 28, 29, 35, 43, 175

labour laws 50, 107, 108
labour unrest 128, 130, 131, 187
Leask, James 193
Lenin ix, 84, 98, 196, 209
Lieven, Prince Paul 29, 31, 33, 34, 39, 47, 139
Lithuania 55, 127
Lockhart, Robert 198
Loxley, Frederick 180
Lugansk 28, 52, 59, 61, 62, 129, 175, 179
Lyttleton, Alfred 100, 165